The Seven Pillars of Wisdom
for Teenagers

A Study Guide of the Seven Core Principles of Wisdom Found in the Book of Proverbs

By

Harry Murphy

Copyright © 2010 by Harry Murphy

The Seven Pillars of Wisdom for Teenagers
A Study Guide of the Seven Core Principles of Wisdom
Found in the Book of Proverbs
by Harry Murphy

Printed in the United States of America

ISBN 9781609576851

All rights reserved solely by the author. The author guarantees all contents are original and do not infringe upon the legal rights of any other person or work. No part of this book may be reproduced in any form without the permission of the author. The views expressed in this book are not necessarily those of the publisher.

Unless otherwise indicated, Bible quotations are taken from The Holy Bible, New International Version. Copyright © 1973, 1978, 1984 by the International Bible Society. Used by permission of Zondervan Publishing House; and The "NIV" and "New International Version" trademarks are registered in the United States Patent and Trademark Office by International Bible Society. Expanded or paraphrased references are the author's own.

www.xulonpress.com

Appreciation

A special word of thanks to my parents, Patricia Lothaire Murphy and Harry B. Murphy Sr., for their lifelong support, instruction and wisdom. To my grandmother, Clifford Tootle Durrence, who said little but taught much in the way of wisdom. To the many, many people—pastors, teachers, youth workers, and counselors—who have shared their wisdom over the years. Thank you Margery Barroll. Also thanks to Sammie Murphy and Jarl K. Waggoner for their assistance with the manuscript. Lastly, thanks to Jack Walton for his encouragement, and the rest of the helpful staff at Xulon Press.

To John Liam Murphy

"A wise son makes a father glad"
Proverbs 10:1

Thanks!

What is more valuable than all the gold and silver in the world, more beautiful than all the pieces of art on earth, and more inspiring than the tallest skyscrapers?

Wisdom

Why?

Wisdom preserves your life, protects your soul, and is the only sure possible means whereby one obtains *CHARACTER*, which in turn brings fulfillment and satisfaction.

*"You who are on the road
must have a code
that you can live by."*

Graham Nash
"Teach Your Children"

"Wisdom has built her house;
she has hewn out its seven pillars."

Proverbs 9:1

Table of Contents

To the Reader xii
Introduction xvii
Pillar 1: Humility: The Supreme Attitude 19
Pillar 2: Carefulness in Companionship 34
Pillar 3: Purity in Sexuality 42
Pillar 4: Diligence at Work 58
Pillar 5: Carefulness in Speech 70
Pillar 6: Simplicity of Lifestyle 78
Pillar 7: Love for the Less Fortunate 86
Concluding Statement
Appendices
    Section I: Helpful Outlines 95
      Appendix A: Living with Greater Humility 97
      Appendix B: Living with Greater Carefulness
        in Companionship 98
      Appendix C: Living with Greater Sexual Purity ... 99
      Appendix D: Living with Greater Diligence in
        Your Work 101
      Appendix E: Living with Greater Control of Your
        Speech 103

Appendix F: Living with Greater Simplicity of
 Lifestyle 105
Appendix G: Living with Greater Love for the Less
 Fortunate 108
Section II: Supplemental Information 111
 Appendix H: The Specific Benefits of Wisdom 113
 Appendix I: A Simple Weekly Schedule for
  Obtaining Greater Wisdom 114
 Appendix J: A Memory System for Obtaining
  Greater Wisdom 116

To the Reader

The Mission Statement of This Book

The mission of this study guide is twofold:

1. To provide the teenager with a concise presentation of the seven essential themes of wisdom found in the book of Proverbs. These **seven[1] principles of wisdom** represent the core wisdom found in the book of Proverbs.
2. To provide concise outlines so that the teenager will be able to "jump-start" his or her adventure into wisdom. Each of these outlines provides practical, everyday activities that the teenager can do in order to walk in the paths of wisdom. Finally, a brief survey of the many benefits or rewards of wisdom are presented in appendix H. This will help the teenager to understand the immense practical value of wisdom.

How to Use This Book

1. As you read this study guide, you will notice a "key verse" that is presented at the beginning of each chapter that covers a specific principle of wisdom. The key verse for a particular pillar of wisdom represents its essence. Before you read a given chapter, it is recommended that you memorize the key verse that is presented at the beginning of the chapter. This will help to fix in your mind a particular principle of wisdom.

2. In each chapter, there is a series of interactive questions to further your understanding of wisdom. Taking the time to answer these questions will expand your discovery and comprehension of wisdom. Furthermore, you are encouraged to keep a journal to *daily* track your thoughts and experiences as you grow in wisdom. This will give you a chance to focus your attention daily on the seven pillars of wisdom. By daily directing your attention to these principles of wisdom, you will increase the likelihood for growth in the ways of wisdom.

The Overall Format of This Book

This book is designed to present the most important material first. Hence, the seven pillars of wisdom are presented first. As in the spirit of the book of Proverbs,[2] the truths of wisdom are presented in a concise manner. Supplementary materials to the seven pillars of wisdom are presented in appendices.

***

NOTES

[1] Hence, the contents of this study guide are arranged around *seven, central principles* found in the book of Proverbs (thus, the title, *The Seven Pillars of Wisdom*). A pillar, by definition, is "an upright column used to support part or all of a structure." For this reason, a pillar is considered to be a core or essential part of a building. Without strong pillars a structure is more susceptible to damage, if not destruction. Likewise, when it comes to building and managing our lives, without constructive principles to live by, we become more susceptible to destructive choices and habits. By incorporating these seven principles or "pillars" into their lives, teenagers will learn not only to think wisely but also to increase the likelihood for experiencing a more secure and satisfying life.

A "pillar," or principle, of wisdom is identified as having fifteen or more references or verses in the book of Wisdom, and can be used by anyone to improve his or her daily life. In the spirit of the book of Proverbs, the presentation of each pillar of wisdom in this book is concise and to the point. The prescriptions for wisdom in life are not to be lost in elaborate or "wordy" dissertations. When it comes to wisdom, beauty is found in brevity of expression. Thus, conciseness of presentation is considered to be essential, providing the student of wisdom with greater time for putting into practice the wisdom so succinctly presented.

[2]Throughout this study guide, the titles *the book of Proverbs, the Proverbs of Solomon, the Book of Wisdom,* and the shortened form, *Proverbs,* are used interchangeably to refer to the same ancient text of wisdom.

Introduction

The greatest need of any teenager is wisdom. With the various pitfalls and challenges teenagers face in today's world, they need all the help they can get. Wisdom not only shows the teenager how to avoid failure and heartache but also how to achieve success and satisfaction in life.

The greatest source of wisdom for teenagers is the book of Proverbs. *In fact, the book of Proverbs is the only book of the Bible written specifically for teenagers.* King Solomon's own introduction to his book of Proverbs directs our attention to the intended audience:

> **These are the wise sayings of Solomon,**
> **David's son, Israel's king—**
> **Written down so we'll know how to live well and right,**
> **to understand what life means and where it's going;**
> **A manual for living,**
> **for learning what's right and just and fair;**
> **To teach the inexperienced the ropes and**
> **give our young people a grasp on reality.**
> (Proverbs 1:1-4)[1]

King Solomon composed the book of Proverbs to, "give *our young people* a grasp on reality." King Solomon wanted to give all young people a good dose of reality therapy. He wanted to teach teenagers how life really works. Today's teenagers and youth have the same tremendous need as those who lived in the time of King

Solomon: *to understand how life or reality works*. Thus, wise King Solomon could be considered the first counselor in history who specifically wrote for the benefit of teenagers and young adults. His collection of guidance and prudent counsel for teenagers is still without equal or peer. The beauty of the seven pillars of wisdom lies in their simplicity. They can be easily understood and applied by anyone. Yet, these simple pillars of wisdom will give any teenager the *power* to bring about positive changes in his or her life. Ultimately, these seven pillars of wisdom are for any teenager who wants to understand life and experience a more successful and satisfying way of living.

Youth pastors and counselors will find the contents of this booklet especially useful in working with teenagers and young adults. The seven pillars of wisdom for teenagers are presented in a clear and concise manner. Interactive questions and practical outlines are provided to facilitate discussions and help teens explore and apply the seven pillars of wisdom to their lives. This book can easily be read in less than an hour, but the constructive and rewarding outcomes that can be derived from the seven pillars of wisdom will last a lifetime.

***

NOTES

[1]*The Message,* translation of the Bible by Eugene H. Peterson. Copyright © 1993, 1994, 1995, 1996, 2000, 2001, 2002.

Pillar 1

Humility: The Supreme Attitude

> "With Pride comes disgrace, but with humility comes wisdom."
> (Proverbs 11:2)

How would you like to get along better with your friends? Would you like to improve your relationships at home with your brothers or sisters? What about your relationships with your parents or your teachers? Could the way you interact with them be in need of constructive change? Would you like to significantly improve your chances for success in life? If your answer to any of these questions is yes, then this chapter concerning humility has been written just for you.

Humility is the first and most important pillar of wisdom for teenagers. Yet, *humility* is a word you normally do not find in casual conversation. It is a word that is rarely, if ever, the central topic at teen gatherings. Moreover, in some circles, the idea of humility is treated with contempt and ridicule. Humility is rarely associated with fame or the status of being a teen celebrity. Most teenagers look for opportunities to display their pride rather than their humility. Facebook, MySpace, and Twitter (and similar internet sites) are all designed to allow the individual to focus on themselves rather than others. In spite of all this, without humility, no significant or meaningful amount of wisdom can be obtained. In fact, humility is required for wisdom to take root, blossom, and bring forth its satisfying fruit (rewards) in our lives. There are no "shortcuts" to wisdom. All other principles of wisdom are dependent upon humility for their existence. Hence, due to the tremendous importance of humility, this introductory section will be more extensive than the other chapters.

The book of Proverbs presents humility as *the key* to gaining wisdom. In fact, humility is a core theme running throughout the book of Proverbs. Proverbs 11:2b states that **"with humility comes wisdom."** First comes humility; then comes wisdom. Humility is the crucial pillar upon which all the other six pillars of wisdom depend for their existence. *In this sense, humility is the foundation for wisdom, and it must be established first in order for the other principles of wisdom to be fully developed.* The high priority of humility cannot be overemphasized when it comes to acquiring wisdom.

The word translated "humility" comes from an ancient Hebrew word, *anah*. *Anah* means to "bow down." The picture portrayed by this ancient Hebrew word is that of a subject who willingly "bows down" on his hands and knees before his king or master. Complete submission of mind, body, heart and soul is implied. *Thus, humility is defined as a deeply submissive way of thinking that significantly affects one's attitudes and actions.* By adopting a submissive or humble mindset, the teenager experiences three beneficial attitudes:

1. A willingness to learn—openness
2. A willingness to listen—attentiveness
3. A willingness to follow—obedience

The first two attitudes of humility go hand in hand: a willingness to learn and a willingness to listen (Proverbs 15:31). These two attributes are similar, yet there are some differences. Willingness to learn is characterized by having an open mind. A closed mind is a sign of pride and arrogance. A closed mind does not facilitate learning. On the other hand, an open mind indicates some degree of humility and a willingness to learn about a subject. Any sincere student of wisdom must first have an open mind. Hence, a willingness to learn is the first trait of humility.

The second attribute of humility, a willingness to listen, refers to focusing our attention on a given subject. Having an open mind to wisdom, in and of itself, is not enough to be an effective student of wisdom. We must be willing to listen to, or focus our attention on, the principles of wisdom in order to maximize our levels of learning. Attentive listening is essential in order to increase our exposure to, and comprehension of, wisdom. The humble teenager is not only open to learning about wisdom but also is willing to carefully listen and meditate on the principles of wisdom.

The third attitude of humility is a willingness to follow. This attitude is crucial if one is to walk in the ways of wisdom. A willingness to follow could be defined as a willingness to act on what one has learned. Listening and learning of wisdom is good, but it is better if one walks in wisdom. Ultimately, humility or submission means walking in the way that one has been instructed. By following or walking in the principles found in Proverbs, the teenager is able to make the most of his or her exposure to wisdom. Significantly, obedience to wisdom brings about the rewards of wisdom. On the other hand, *knowledge that is not applied is essentially knowledge that is wasted.* Hence, humility has a behavioral dimension or component. True humility is not just an attitude; it also involves action. By humbly walking in the ways of wisdom, the teenager will experience the rewards of wisdom. Twelve specific benefits of wisdom are outlined in appendix H.

Along with changes in attitudes, humility also brings about changes in your thought patterns. ***The prideful or foolish teenager is continually thinking about himself***—what *he* has done (the past), what *he* is doing (the present), and what *he* will be doing (the future).

The prideful teenager's existence is centered on pleasure. Yet this type of self-centered thinking inevitably leads to dissatisfaction.[1] On the other hand, the humble teenager makes it a habit to think about others. The humble teenager does not view his life as being the only focus of life, but rather a wonderful gift from God. He recognizes that everything he has ultimately comes from God. Moreover, the humble teenager focuses on helping others meet their basic needs. This often begins by sharing wisdom with those in need. Hence, the wise teenager centers his existence on those principles of wisdom that are helpful both to himself and others.

Another important shift in the thought patterns of the humble teen is a daily focus on the principle of sowing and reaping. Humility recognizes that all of life is based on the principle of sowing and reaping. "Sowing and reaping" is a phrase used to describe why things happen—the process of actions and reactions (consequences). In everyday speech, the term *Karma* is often used to refer to the consequences of one's thoughts and actions. A fundamental aspect of gaining wisdom is the awareness that all of our thoughts and actions have consequences—whether for better or for worse. Note that the principle of Karma, or sowing and reaping, is clearly taught in the book of Proverbs.

"He who sows wickedness reaps trouble." (Proverbs 22:8a)

"A person's own folly ruins his life." (Proverbs 19:3)

The book of Proverbs makes it clear: those who sow destructive attitudes and behaviors will reap unpleasant circumstances; on the other hand, those who sow constructive attitudes and actions will reap pleasing circumstances and emotions. The humble teen recognizes the reality of Karma in everyday life. "What goes around, comes around." This recognition can save a person from much trouble and grief.

Understanding Karma will help to bring about right thinking. Right thinking involves thinking in terms of wisdom. Right thinking will bring about right actions. Right actions will result in positive emotions and the development of character (stability or consistency of wise actions). And character ultimately will result in a destiny of achievement, honor, and satisfaction. Moreover, right thoughts and actions involve thinking about the needs and wants of others. Right thinking involves spending less time centered on pleasing oneself and more time helping others. Wrong thinking (selfish thinking) will result in harmful behaviors and feelings, both to oneself and to others. For example, self-centered thoughts and actions increase conflict in relationships. Selfish thinking tends to ignore or minimize the thoughts and feelings of others and thus causes conflicts. In the long run, selfish behaviors will result in a life of regret and dissatisfaction. The humble teenager, therefore, recognizes and submits himself to the law of sowing and reaping. ***Do good, and good things happen; do bad, and bad things happen.*** The wise teenager avoids selfish thoughts and actions. He recognizes and appreciates his need for other people. He acts as if everyone he meets is part of his extended family. He knows that he cannot help another without helping himself; contrariwise, he also knows that if he harms another, he is also harming himself. The humble teenager recognizes that Karma is an important part of humility that must be daily recognized and used in order to achieve a life of fulfillment. To ignore this vital principle of sowing and reaping is to sow the seeds of one's own dissatisfaction.

Along with the awareness of Karma, the humble teenager is also aware of nature (all the elements of life on this planet). This is part of being less self-focused and more attentive to one's surroundings. More specifically, the wise teenager is acutely aware of the lessons that can be learned from nature. The primary lesson of nature can be summed up in one word: *life*. All of nature is teeming with life. This is the business of nature. The Discovery Channel's popular series *Life* emphasizes this reality. Everything on this planet is centered on life. The humble person recognizes that nature's central focus is life.

This awareness concerning nature can be broken down into two fundamental processes: (1) the procreation or the generation of life, and (2) the protection or the safeguarding of life. All other elements or processes in nature are secondary to these two processes. This is what planet earth is fundamentally and ultimately about: creating and sustaining life. The humble teenager seeks to find his or her role in these two overriding processes. The humble teen seeks not to fight against these two strong currents of nature but rather to join in and flow with them. The wise teenager daily recognizes that his or her life is dependent upon these two fundamental processes of nature. The wise teenager flows with these two processes and in doing so experiences greater peace and joy.

Ultimately, a humble attitude is indicated by a deep appreciation for all aspects of life on earth. The humble teenager realizes that his life is the product of others, beginning with his or her parents. But the teenager's appreciation for others does not end there. The humble teenager realizes that hundreds, if not thousands, of individuals have added to his or her well-being. This includes people from the past who have strived to make our world and our lives better today. All the societal and technological advances are the result of the thoughtfulness and hard work of thousands. The evolution of society and civilization was not by happenstance but by the choices and perseverance of thousands of people from the past who worked to enhance civilization for future generations. Hence, the humble teenager strives to recognize and honor the efforts of all who have labored to made society more secure, livable, and enjoyable.

The humble teen is also appreciative of those people who are presently working for his or her benefit. First and foremost, the humble teen is appreciative of those parents who have tried to prepare him or her for life. (Unfortunately, some parents do not teach nor practice wisdom with their children.) Parents are not perfect. Indeed, parents are under a tremendous amount of financial and emotional stress; however, they are greatly pleased when their children express appreciation for all that they try to do. Expressing gratitude to one's parents is a great way to reinforce constructive parental behaviors. Although honor and appreciation should start with parents, it also should extend beyond the family. A general attitude of appreciation should go to anyone in our neighborhood and society who is working to make our lives more secure and satisfying. This includes people in the medical fields, such as doctors and nurses, medical technologists, secretaries, and their coworkers. Also, people who are employed in schools, such as teachers, counselors, social workers, and their support personnel, are to be recognized for their hard work. People who are involved in law enforcement, fire fighting, and emergency response are essential for our security and well being. Those who honorably serve in the armed services should be appreciated for their service to our country. Also, the wise teenager will recognize all those individuals who are working at the local, state, and federal levels, providing for us a stable and secure environment. Along with these people, the humble teenager recognizes the hundreds, and in some cases thousands, of workers who are employed by the state and local government to make our communities safe and pleasant—from sanitation workers to traffic engineers to our mayors and aldermen. All of these civil servants are vital to our community and society as a whole. *In the end, the attitude of appreciation is a core part of humility,* beginning with the honoring of wise parents and extending to gratitude for the humblest civil servant. By remembering and honoring those who make our lives more secure and successful, we begin to recognize the extreme importance of other people. Humility emphasizes and values humanity. Thus, for the humble teenager, there is a deep appreciation for the multitude of people, both from the past and in the present, who are actively working to make life more safe and satisfying.

Next, it also must be said that an attitude of appreciation is not only due to people but also to the earth in which we live. Just as wisdom is a rare jewel among works of literature, so also is our planet a singular, unique jewel among the planets. *No other known planet among the thousands, if not millions, that exist in the universe have proven to come close to earth's life-generating properties.* Earth is truly the only *known* planet in the entire universe that so encourages and supports life. In fact, as we have mentioned earlier, planet earth's most prominent focus is that of generating and supporting life. Thus, the humble teenager is daily aware of this and is greatly appreciative of the life-giving processes that are found throughout planet earth. The humble teen understands that all of the life-giving processes on earth interact together, contributing to his survival and well-being. *With this in mind, the humble teenager focuses on taking care of the earth. He or she stresses the conservation of the earth and its resources, rather than the impulsive and wasteful con-*

sumption of its resources. A simple and less materialistic lifestyle is embraced by the wise teenager. The humble teenager does not desire the biggest home or the newest car. Rather, he or she is more devoted to conserving and preserving the life-giving elements that are a part of earth. For the wise, taking care of the earth, which has been so supportive of the human race, is important. The humble person is focused on being thankful for, and protective of, all of the magnificent, life-supporting processes of earth.

Therefore, the humble teenager has a multitude of reasons to be thankful. Thankfulness and appreciation are central components of humility. Furthermore, in the final analysis, every teenager has a multitude of reasons—all of those previously mentioned—to be thankful to God. Humility allows us to clearly see that God has provided for our every need. God has given us a rare jewel of a planet to inhabit, and He has given us an amazing potential to help us provide for ourselves. The human creature is an awesome creation, both in its design and abilities. In fact, one of the most basic beliefs of the Judeo-Christian tradition is that *man and women were originally created in the very image of God.* What an awesome thought. No other part of creation can claim this distinction and honor. This is an awesome truth that the humble teenager can celebrate daily. Accepting this belief can only enhance a teenager's self-esteem or self-worth. Also, by looking at others as being created in the very image of God, makes us more inclined to be respectful and compassionate toward them. Viewing every human being as a reflection of God's image can only give greater value to each person we meet. With this attitude we are more prone to view everyone with a certain awe, which in turn can lead to mutually fulfilling relationships and a greater likelihood for peaceful coexistence. In addition, the humble teenager realizes that God has provided the wisdom necessary to experience life on earth in a fulfilling and abundant manner. God has given us wise people, both past and present, to help us make this journey called life more rewarding. From this perspective, God is the ultimate Provider. Given the tremendous challenges that each teenager faces in life, a mind-set that includes a benevolent and loving Provider is significantly beneficial.

In conclusion, Humility is the door that allows us to have an appreciative mind-set. The humble teenager is thankful for a multitude of blessings that are found in his or her life. There is no other attitude more needed today than humility. This is because humility is the central gateway through which one obtains the fullness of wisdom. For the teenager, humility is *the key* to acquiring the other virtues of wisdom. In this sense, it is the key to *character development.* Humility is necessary in order to avoid pride and the negative consequences that it brings. An attitude of humility brings about a lifestyle that is both successful and fulfilling. Humility is the central means for obtaining the "good life." Wisdom promotes life and peace. Relationships become more satisfying. Work becomes more productive. Emotions are set at peace. Humility allows us to truly be appreciative of our lives, our parents, our relationships, our work, our planet, other people, and all the life-supporting elements within nature. Most importantly, humility allows us to be appreciative of God. Hence, humility is the ultimate mind-set through which a great many spiritual, emotional, and material blessings are realized and by which the door to greater wisdom is fully opened.

To further your understanding of the first pillar of wisdom—humility—answer the following questions.

Questions for Further Research and Application

1. How are the concepts of humility and appreciation connected?
___
___
___
___

2. From what you have read in this chapter, what are three basic constructive attitudes that spring from humility?
___
___
___
___

3. How is the concept of sowing and reaping (Karma) connected to humility?

_____
_____
_____
_____

4. How is the honoring of wise authority figures an important part of humility?

_____
_____
_____
_____

5. How does humility recognize and stress the importance of other people?

_____
_____
_____
_____

6. Why is an attitude of gratitude a central element of humility?

_____
_____
_____
_____

7. How will humility help you get along better with your peers?

_____
_____
_____
_____

8. Will humility help you with your relationships with your parents? How?

_____
_____

The Seven Pillars of Wisdom for Teenagers

9. In what ways does humility help you honor your parents?

10. How will humility help you become a better student at school?

11. How will humility help you become a better worker on your job?

12. Will humility help you appreciate your teachers at school? If your answer is "yes," then how will you show greater appreciation to your teachers?

13. Humility accepts the idea that all people are created in God's image. How does humility help you to be more accepting of yourself?

14. Will humility improve your relationships with your parents? How?

15. Does humility help you to appreciate the wonders of planet earth? If your answer is "yes," then how can you show greater appreciation for God's creation/earth and its precious resources?

16. How does seeing everyone as a creation of God—created in His image—help you to maintain a humble and appreciative attitude towards others?

17. Pride is the opposite of humility. Read Proverbs 11:2. What does disgrace mean to you? Again look at Proverbs 11:2. How can this verse apply to your life?

18. Look at the words *pride* and *sin*. What letter at the center of both of these words pinpoints the core problem that all human beings suffer from? How does living solely for "I" negatively affect your life?

The Seven Pillars of Wisdom for Teenagers

_____
_____

19. Does pride bring strife or harmony in our relationships with our friends and family? How?

_____
_____
_____
_____

20. Someone has described a prideful person as "a know-it-all who tells it all!" What does this descriptive phrase mean to you?

_____
_____
_____
_____

21. In what constructive ways will humility impact your life?

_____
_____
_____
_____
_____
_____
_____
_____
_____

  In conclusion, a humble teenager has much to gain in life. Humility is the foundation for building a life of wisdom. Humility will constructively affect your relationships, especially with your family members and your friends. Humility helps us to make the right choices in life, whereas pride prompts us to make the wrong choices. Pride results in conflicts, despair, and depression. ***Pride brings out the worst in anyone and ultimately brings about failure*** *and shame. On the other hand, Humility will bring out your best.* Humility will allow you to experience greater gratitude and thankfulness for all things. This in turn helps to protect you from depression and stress related illnesses. A grateful and cheerful heart will boost your immune system, resulting in greater health. As king Solomon stated, **"A cheerful heart is good medicine."** (Proverbs 17:22) In the end, humility not only produces greater health but also greater harmony in your relationships. Humility, rather than pride, is the sure pathway to greater peace, joy and blessings in your life.[2]

- Review and memorize the key verse for the first pillar of wisdom.

"With pride comes disgrace, but with humility comes wisdom." (Proverbs 11:2)

- Weekly study schedule: Every Sunday review and meditate on the first pillar of wisdom. Meditate on it throughout the day, and look for opportunities to put it into practice throughout the week.
- Additional verses in Proverbs concerning humility: 1:7; 3:34; 8:13; 9:10; 11:2; 14:12, 26, 27; 15:33; 16:5, 18, 19; 18:12; 19:23; 21:29; 22:4; 28:14; 29:23.
- See Appendix A for an outline of behaviors that will help you to implement humility into your daily life.

***

NOTES

[1] Many years ago there was a number one pop song recorded by the Rolling Stones entitled, "I Can't Get No Satisfaction." Over forty times in this song the singer references himself by using the pronouns *I* or *me*. The person this song is about is self-centered and completely self-absorbed. Thus, according to the law of Karma, it should be no surprise that he "can't get no satisfaction." This person is living in his own hell as a result of his self-centered existence.

Karma teaches that the person who is self-centered and self-focused will never realize any lasting personal fulfillment or satisfaction.

[2]Overview of the value of Humility for teenagers
- **I. Psychological benefits of humility**
    - A. Higher self-esteem
    - B. Greater self-confidence
    - C. A positive identity
    - D. Greater internal peace due to less conflict with one's conscience
- **II. Social benefits of humility (greater peace in one's relationships)**
    - A. Improved relationships with family
    - B. Improved relationships with friends
    - C. Improved relationships with workmates
    - D. If married, improved relationship with one's spouse
- **III. Career benefits of humility**
    - A. Better attitude toward work.
    - B. Increased productivity
    - C. Increased likelihood for promotions
    - D. Increased likelihood for financial rewards

Pillar 2

Carefulness in Companionship

"He who walks with the wise grows wise,
but a companion of fools suffers harm."
(Proverbs 13:20)

The teen years are a time when young people start to expand their social network. Their peers take on greater importance. Teenagers often spend more time apart from their family as they develop new friendships. And this is often considered to be a typical part of a teenager's growth and development. The teenage years can be a time of tremendous growth—physically, socially, and mentally. It is also a time of greater challenges and responsibilities. Indeed, one of the most important challenges of this time period is that of choosing the right friends.

During the teenage years, young people seek to develop a clearer picture of their identity, a sense of their individuality. And it is during those years that we often look to our peers for the answers to who we are. How we define ourselves can be strongly influenced by our peers. Moreover, our identity includes formulating beliefs about what is right and wrong. *A teenager's standards for evaluating right and wrong are often influenced by his or her friends.* This influence can occur subconsciously, without one's awareness. Thus, teenagers need to be mindful of how their peers can shape their identity and moral development. This awareness of the role of peer pressure is an important part of growing in wisdom.

Teenagers need to always keep in mind that their friends can influence greatly how they feel about themselves. A teenager must choose those friends who would not only offer emotional support but also provide wisdom for living. The right kind of friends can lead to many positive outcomes in a teen's life. On the other hand, having the wrong kind of friends will lead to negative choices and consequences. Indeed, a person's future success will be greatly affected by the person's choice of friends.

In summary, this second pillar of wisdom emphasizes the importance of choosing the right friends. Choosing the right friends is necessary in order to experience a successful and satisfying life. As teenagers, your attitudes about yourself, as well as your daily actions, will be highly influenced by your friends. **Therefore, this pillar of wisdom counsels you to** *be extremely careful in choosing your friends.* **How? Look for friends who try to follow the seven pillars of wisdom. You will never regret having wise friends.**

To further your understanding of the second pillar of wisdom—choosing wise friends—answer the following questions.

Questions for Further Research and Application

1. How will your friends affect your attitude towards wisdom?

___
___
___
___

2. In what ways can a bad friend subconsciously influence your behavior?

_____
_____
_____
_____

3. The famous Greek philosopher Socrates tells us, "Be slow to fall into friendship." Why should you be slow or cautious in forming new friendships?

_____
_____
_____
_____

4. If we want to be successful in life, then what kind of people should we actively seek as friends? Why?

_____
_____
_____
_____

5. Our companions influence our beliefs, behavior, and lifestyles. Given this reality, should you be careless or extremely careful in choosing your friends? How can you exercise greater carefulness in choosing your friends?

_____
_____
_____
_____

6. In seeking the companionship of a spouse, should one seek for a spouse who is wise or foolish? What are some characteristics to look for in a potential spouse?

_____
_____
_____

7. Read Proverbs 1:10-19.
   "My sons, if sinners entice you, do not give in to them. If they say, *'come along with us*; let's lie in wait for someone's blood, Let's waylay some harmless soul; Let's swallow them alive, like the grave, and whole, like those who go down to the pit; we will get all sorts of valuable things and fill our houses with plunder; throw in your lot with us, and we will share a common purse.' My son *do not go along with them*, do not set foot on their paths; for their feet rush into sin, they are swift to shed blood. How useless to spread a net in full view of all the birds! These men lie in wait for their own blood; they waylay only themselves! Such is the end of all who go after ill-gotten gain, it takes away the lives of those who get it."

What are these important verses teaching you about the dangers of the wrong kind of peer group? What is this passage telling us about the dangers of a gang?

_____
_____
_____
_____

8. Note carefully verses 18 and 19 of Proverbs 1.
   "These men lie in wait for their own blood; they waylay only themselves!
   Such is the end of all who go after ill-gotten gain; it takes away the lives of those who get it."

What ultimately happens to those who join gangs?

_____
_____
_____
_____

9. Read Proverbs 13:20.
> **"He who walks with the wise grows wise,
> but a companion of fools suffers harm."**

What happens to those who listen to and follow fools? On the other hand, according to this verse, what happens to a teenager who keeps company with the wise?

_____
_____
_____
_____

10. Will making friends with a troublemaker or lawbreaker at school help you or harm you in your efforts to get an education?

_____
_____
_____
_____

11. One of the greatest dangers of making friends with the foolish is that we will learn their behaviors. We all want to be accepted. The only way to be accepted by a foolish person is to adopt their attitudes and lifestyle. What negative outcomes will this have for us? First, read Proverbs 22:24-25.
> **"Do not make friends with a hot-tempered man; do not
> associate with one easily angered, or you may learn his
> ways and get yourself ensnared."**

What do these verses mean to you?

_____
_____
_____
_____

12. How will associating with an unwise or foolish coworker affect your performance at work?

13. How will "hanging out" with the unwise affect your attitude toward life?

14. Read Proverbs 15:22.
   "Plans fail for a lack of counsel, but with many wise advisers they succeed."

If we want to be a success in life, then what kind of friends should we seek advice from—the wise or the foolish? Why?

15. Where would be a good place to find a wise friend? Would you be more likely to find a wise friend in a church or in a bar? Why?

16. As applied to dating, should you be dating someone who does not live according to the principles of wisdom (especially these seven core principles of wisdom)? Why?

17. How can dating an unwise or foolish person lead to disastrous consequences?

18. The person you are dating may be the person you marry. Should you expect to find happiness if you are married to an unwise or foolish person? Why?

19. Read the following statement: "The best way to harm yourself is to hang with unwise people." What does this mean?

20. On the other hand, write out your reaction to the following statement: "The best way to love yourself is to hang with wise friends."

21. In what constructive ways will wise friends make your life better and improve your chances for success?

To summarize, one of the most important factors affecting the life of a teenager is his or her friends. Wise King Solomon recognized the tremendous dangers of being with the wrong group and strongly warned his own sons to avoid them. Unwise friends will have a negative impact on your attitudes and actions. As a teenager, your friends can have a tremendous influence on your growth in wisdom. Thus, a high degree of caution needs to be exercised in choosing your friends. *If you choose to associate with unwise friends, then you will more likely engage in foolish behaviors, with the results being greater degrees of regret and dissatisfaction. On the other hand, if you choose wise and compassionate friends, you will experience greater wisdom and success in life, and this will bring about greater levels of personal satisfaction.*

- Review and memorize the key verse for the second pillar of wisdom.

"He who walks with the wise grows wise, but a companion of fools suffers harm." (Proverbs 13:20)

- Weekly study schedule: Every Monday review and meditate on the second pillar of wisdom. Meditate on it throughout the day, and look for opportunities to put it into practice throughout the week.
- Additional verses in Proverbs on carefulness in companionship: 1:10-19; 11:14; 14:7; 15:22; 16:19; 18:24; 20:18-19; 21:16; 22:5, 24; 23:20-21; 24:6, 21; 28:7; 29:3, 12, 24.
- See appendix B: Living with Greater Carefulness in Companionship

Pillar 3

Purity in Sexuality

"This teaching (of sexual purity) is a light . . . keeping you from the immoral person (the person who is sexually unrestrained)."
(Proverbs 6:23-24)

Teenagers have a natural and normal interest in sex and reproduction. This is normal. Most teenagers take a heightened interest in their peer group and especially the opposite sex. Interestingly, the book of Proverbs has a lot to say about sexual behavior and its consequences. In fact, Proverbs speaks more about sexuality than any other specific subject. To walk in wisdom is to have a full understanding of the highly influential role that sex plays in our lives and in any relationship. From the standpoint of wisdom, the overriding focus is on sexual purity. In fact, two chapters of Proverbs (chapters

5 and 7) are exclusively devoted to the idea of sexual purity. For the teenager, this understanding is crucial. Because of the importance of sexual purity, this section will be more extensive than some of the other chapters.

Maintaining sexual purity is one of the central goals of wisdom. It is also one of the central objectives of wisdom during adolescence. During your teenage years, your body is going through a period of fantastic growth and development. During this period of growth, hormones are released to help facilitate growth. In addition, these hormones increase your interest in the opposite sex. This is normal! Yet, wisdom is needed in order to protect yourself from harmful choices during the teenage years. You need wisdom in order to have the right attitude and the right actions when interacting with the opposite sex.

Sexual purity rests on the belief that God created sex to be enjoyed within the protective and nurturing boundaries of marriage. Sex is not "dirty" or bad when used in its proper place. Sex within marriage is a beautiful expression of the love that a couple shares for one another. Sex is symbolic of the commitment and unity of the marriage of two people. Hence, sexual purity does not involve the idea of avoiding sex but rather enjoying it in its proper time and place. From the perspective of wisdom, the proper time and place for sex is marriage.

Indeed, sex helps to strengthen the marital relationship between a man and woman. Usually, when a couple experiences sex, an emotional bond is created. This is crucial for teenagers to understand. If a teenage couple experiences sex before marriage, they become emotionally bonded to one another. They may think they are ready for all the responsibilities of marriage before they are mature enough for all of the duties and responsibilities of marriage. Marriage normally involves the birth of children. Yet, having and providing for children is a tremendous responsibility. Teenagers need to realize the connection between sex and the responsibility of having children. *The great joy of having children is matched by the tremendous responsibilities that come with children.* Thus, sex needs to find its proper time and place in marriage. Sexual purity will not only protect your life as a teenager, but it will also benefit your marriage in the future.

Thus, the way of wisdom involves reserving sex for marriage. By reserving sex for marriage, the teenager will be free from worrying about all the responsibilities involved in marriage and the raising of children. Resisting premarital sex will relieve you of many stressors (such as an unplanned and unwanted pregnancy). Moreover, by saving sex for marriage you will become more fully devoted to your responsibilities as a teenager. You will have more time to focus on developing the life skills necessary for a successful, future career. Furthermore, sexual purity will help you to increase your self-esteem and feelings of personal satisfaction, thus minimizing feelings of inferiority and depression. In summary, this principle of sexual purity has many benefits[1] that will bring greater satisfaction to your life, protecting you in your teenager years as well as in your adult life.

To further your understanding of the third pillar of wisdom—sexual purity—answer the following questions. Additional information is provided with the questions below to stimulate thought and discussion.

Questions for Further Research and Application

1. Why is it important to avoid going out with a person who emphasizes the physical (sexual) side of dating?

_____
_____
_____
_____

2. What are some of the most significant drawbacks of engaging in premarital sex?

_____
_____
_____
_____

There are many negative consequences for those who ignore the principle of sexual purity. It is important that we take a moment to become aware of the downside of sexual permissiveness. Strangely enough, this downside to premarital sex is rarely, if ever, presented in the mass media. As you will see, many of these problems are serious. By saving sex until marriage, you will protect yourself from these problems, along with the stress and worry that is associated with premarital sex. The stressors of premarital sex include the following:

- Premarital sex increases the likelihood of sexually transmitted diseases and/or infections.
- Premarital sex increases the possibility of an abortion due to an unplanned pregnancy.
- Premarital sex increases the possibility of having to give up a child for adoption due to an unplanned pregnancy.
- Premarital sex increases the likelihood of a premature marriage. A successful marriage takes a significant degree of maturity. A premature marriage increases the possibility of children before both parties are ready for the responsibilities of marriage. One of the most unsatisfying situations in life is a marriage where neither individual is mature enough to handle the daily responsibilities required to make the marriage mutually fulfilling. A "rushed marriage" often leads to a "ruined marriage."
- Lastly, premarital sex can lead to clinical depression and anxiety. Any of the above mentioned negative consequences of premarital sex can lead to clinical emotional issues. Also, a guilty conscience will compound one's level of depression. Chronic clinical depression or anxiety can ultimately lead to drug abuse and/or suicide.

3. Does the pleasure of having premarital sex outweigh the drawbacks? Explain:
_____
_____
_____
_____

4. As a teenager, what are some constructive alternatives you can engage in rather than premarital sex?

_____
_____
_____
_____

Look at the following list of positive activities. Which of the following five constructive activities could you use to avoid premarital sex?

- Focusing more on schoolwork and good grades
- Getting involved in exercise and/or sports
- Getting involved in artistic expression—painting, poetry, writing, or music
- Getting a part-time job to make extra money
- Getting involved in helping others (see pillar number 7)

5. What reasons do you think are the most valid for avoiding a physical (sexual) relationship with another teenager? (You may use some of the consequences that were listed earlier in this chapter.)

_____
_____
_____
_____

6. What are some of the negative outcomes of having a physical relationship with another teenager?

_____
_____
_____
_____

7. What will happen to your reputation if others find out that you are engaged in premarital sex?

_____
_____

8. What will happen to self-esteem if you engage in premarital sex?

Another important reason to avoid premarital sex is that it can become a bad habit that may continue after you are married. Those who engaged in premarital sex often find it hard to remain pure after marriage. Once a pattern of behavior has been established, it is hard to change it when you become an adult. Learning to control our sexual desires is something that should be done before we are married, not afterwards. *What we do in our youth often becomes habit in adulthood.* If one is promiscuous before marriage, there is a greater chance of being promiscuous after marriage. In other words, past behavior is often a good indicator of future behavior. *To minimize or avoid the temptation for sexual impurity after marriage, one needs to stay sexually pure before marriage.*

9. In what ways will your future marriage be more special if you choose not to engage in premarital sex now as a teenager?

Young men should be especially aware of the dangers of pornography as it relates to premarital sex. Pornography distorts one's thinking about sex. It implies that sex without a strong commitment (marriage) is all right. Second, it primarily portrays a woman as a sexual object for the pleasure of the man. The sexual satisfaction of the woman is often minimized, if not outright ignored. In pornography, the implied message is that the sexual desires of the man are to predominate. This type of mind-set completely ignores the emotional and physical needs of the woman. Moreover, pornography often shapes a man's mind to think that his wife must look perfect in order to elicit his sexual interest. This is both unnatural and unrealistic. Pornography puts an unbalanced view of what a relationship is all about. A marriage is not mainly about sex, but about working together as a team to raise a family and leave a legacy for your family. A relationship is about a commitment of two individuals working toward mutual partnership and mutual fulfillment. Ultimately, a marriage is designed to honor and glorify God who instituted marriage shortly after creation (cf. Genesis 2:18—25). To focus primarily on the physical side of a relationship is to set yourself up for frustration, disappointment and ultimately a marriage destine for failure.

Why is a focus on the physical dimension of a relationship a recipe for failure? To begin with, the physical side is usually the first to go in any relationship. For most couples, the morning after the honeymoon is the time that we start to see the real physical side of our spouse. The groom's hair is no longer neatly combed, and his beard is starting to grow. The cologne has lost its impact. The bride's curls have long since vanished, and the rosy cheeks and enchanting eyes have somehow disappeared. Ultimately, we all lose some of our physical attractiveness. For a relationship to last, it must be based on something other than just physical attraction. Lasting relationships must have a spiritual foundation.

Another important aspect of sexual purity is that of being careful of what we look at or read. The mass media does not promote sexual purity. In fact, the mass media tends to promote sexual permissiveness and other forms of foolishness. There are also magazines, movies, and books that portray sexual contact as being just a normal, casual physical desire that should be fulfilled whenever the occasion presents itself. You need to be careful to avoid these types of media so that you are not be deceived into thinking that premarital sex is good or beneficial.[2] (The mass media is not interested in spreading wisdom or developing your happiness. The goal of the mass media is not to impart wisdom to you but to make money from selling the greatest number of commercials that will appeal to the masses.)

10. How does the mass media portray premarital sex? Does the mass media ever portray the negative side to premarital sex?

_____
_____
_____
_____

11. What should be the man's role in preventing premarital sex?

_____
_____
_____
_____

12. How does pornography distort the proper place that sex has within a relationship?

_____
_____
_____
_____

13. How does pornography work against the concept of a traditional marriage?

_____
_____
_____
_____

14. How does pornography portray the role of the woman in a relationship?

_____
_____
_____
_____

15. What are the dangers of a relationship if it is primarily defined in terms of sex?

Another aspect of applying wisdom to the area of sex has to do with associating with those who are not careful about their involvement in sex. The book of Proverbs has extensive warnings to teenagers or young men about avoiding women who treat sex casually (especially loose women, prostitutes, and the adulteress; read Proverbs 6:23-26).

> **"For these commands are a lamp, this teaching is a light ... keeping you from the immoral woman, from the smooth tongue of the wayward wife."**
> **(Proverbs 6:23-24)**

These are women who are willing to indulge in premarital sex for attention or in an effort to control men. These women have ignored the sanctity of sex. They are living for the physical pleasure of the moment, ignoring the pain and dissatisfaction brought on by their conscience. The "loose" woman is more than eager to pull a young teenager down to her level. By engaging in sex with the loose woman, you will reap many negative consequences. (Besides those consequences listed above, also read chapters 5 and 7 of the book of Proverbs.) Loose women are to be avoided by those who want to experience a truly fulfilling marriage.

For teenage girls, it also should be emphasized that "loose" men—those who do not treat sex as something sacred—need to be avoided. If you associate with friends who do not hold sex in high esteem, then you are likely to find you own attitude about sex compromised. This point was also emphasized during the discussion of maintaining wise friends, the second pillar of wisdom.

16. Why is it wise not to date a "loose" or promiscuous person?

17. Type in "sexually transmitted diseases" on Google. What are some of the sexually transmitted diseases a person can catch by engaging in premarital sex?

18. Since there is no known cure for some of these diseases, how should this affect our attitudes toward premarital sex?

19. Some sexually transmitted diseases can result in infertility. How should this reality affect our thinking toward premarital sex?

20. The woman needs to remember that she also has responsibilities when it comes to dating. She must not engage in activities that will encourage or allow premarital sex to occur. What activities should the female avoid?

21. The bottom line to premarital sex is that it has no real benefits. If sex is engaged in before marriage, there are many destructive conse-

quences that can occur. In what constructive ways will sexual purity affect your life?

_____
_____
_____
_____
_____
_____

In summary, sexual purity can spare the teenager a multitude of problems. There are many benefits[3] for those who save themselves for marriage. Staying sexually pure is a win/win situation. In other words, you will not only save yourself from the possibility of diseases, as well as emotional depression, but you will also increase your chances for enjoying a more meaningful marriage. Most men do not want to marry a woman who is sexually loose. Most men respect and value the woman who reserves sex for marriage. By saving yourself for marriage, you will be viewed as a more valuable and desirable future mate. Moreover, by maintaining sexual purity, sex in your marriage will take on greater meaning and enjoyment. For those who want to make their marriage the best, sexual purity is essential.

In closing, it can be stated that sexual purity before marriage is a *high standard.* But like other high standards in life—the honor roll, high honor roll, Rhodes Scholar, outstanding athlete—it offers the greatest rewards in life for those who are willing to put forth the extra effort to attain and maintain it. *The gold medals go only to those who can jump over the highest bar, not the lowest. If you set low standards for yourself in the area of sex, you will not experience the greatest rewards and satisfaction in life.*

The clear counsel of Proverbs and wisdom is to keep oneself pure before marriage. For the teenager there are many health-related benefits for saving sex for marriage. By maintaining a high moral standard concerning sex, the teenager is setting the foundation for a clear conscience before God and a wonderful future marriage that is truly satisfying and fulfilling.

- Review and memorize the key verse for the third pillar of wisdom.

> **"This teaching (of sexual purity) is a light ... keeping you from the immoral person" (the person who is sexually loose or permissive)."**
> **(Proverbs 6:23-24)**

- Weekly study schedule: Every Tuesday review and meditate on the third pillar of wisdom. Meditate on it throughout the day, and look for opportunities to put it into practice throughout the week.
- Additional passages and verses in Proverbs on sexual purity: 2:16-19; 5:1-23; 6:24-35; 7:1-27; 11:29; 23:27-28; 31:3, 30

***

NOTES

[1]The benefits of maintaining sexual purity include the following.

(1) By avoiding premarital sex, you will not need to worry about health problems. Remember, some sexually transmitted diseases are fatal. Other problems, such as genital herpes and genital warts, can be long lasting, extremely embarrassing, and painful. Currently, sexually transmitted diseases are not only a hassle and a discomfort, but they can also be life threatening.

(2) By avoiding premarital sex, your objectivity about marrying the right person is not clouded. Premarital sex not only physically bonds you to another person, but it also emotionally bonds you to another. Premarital sex puts more responsibility on a teenager to marry. Remember that teenagers are not mature enough for all of the responsibilities involved in marriage.

(3) By avoiding premarital sex, you do not have to worry about whether you are pregnant or not. (As for boys, by avoiding premarital sex, you will not have to worry about whether you have gotten a girl pregnant). The only pregnancy prevention technique that is 100 percent guaranteed is abstinence. The fear of pregnancy is a major

stressor for any teenager and will negatively affect your relationships and responsibilities at home, school, and work.

(4) By avoiding premarital sex, you will not have an unplanned pregnancy. An unplanned pregnancy, and subsequent child, will bring on tremendous responsibilities for which you are not ready. *Educational and career goals will be shattered.* An unplanned pregnancy increases the temptation for an abortion or the likelihood of giving up a child for adoption. Either of these options can lead to post-traumatic stress and long-lasting emotional issues. Thus, an unplanned pregnancy can cause a lifetime of chronic depression and/or regret.

(5) Sexual purity allows you to have greater objectivity in your dating relationships. Sexual purity allows you to make decisions based on facts and wisdom, rather than on your emotions. Mover, by avoiding premarital sex, breaking up with a person you are dating is easier. This means that there is less of a chance of being emotionally hurt when one of you decides to date other people. Thus, by avoiding premarital sex, you will not feel excessively bonded to any one person in particular, and you will save yourself from excessive emotional pain. *By avoiding premarital sex you are saying "yes" to emotional freedom.*

(6) By avoiding premarital sex, you won't feel pressured to marry too early. Teenagers who engage in premarital sex tend to feel that they are "adults" and that they are ready for marriage. In fact, engaging in premarital sex is a sign of immaturity—indicating one is not ready for marriage and its responsibilities. First things first. First focus on your education and setting the foundation for a successful career; then set your sights on marriage. Sex should be the last area that a couple develops in their relationship and that only after the wedding.

(7) By avoiding premarital sex, your self-esteem will be higher. By avoiding premarital sex you will not experience the guilt that comes from hiding something from your family. And once your "friends" find out that you have been having premarital sex, they will not keep it a secret. A promiscuous or pregnant teen gets more "news time" in the local school and neighborhood than the assassination of the president. And once the "news" is out, the boys who show

an interest in you will expect only one thing—easy sex. Premarital sex will bring with it a negative reputation, and this significantly contributes to poor self-esteem. Thus, avoiding premarital sex can help you avoid a bad reputation, depression, and low self-worth.

(8) From a spiritual perspective, by abstaining from premarital sex, you will be living according to the wonderful plan God has for your life—sex within a commitment of marriage. Sexual purity allows you to live according to your God-given conscience. Thus, your conscience will be at rest. You will be at peace. You will sleep better at night. You will not have to worry about the negative consequences of premarital sex. The more you learn to follow your conscience, the greater will be your daily contentment. Try it and experience greater peace!

(9) By avoiding premarital sex, you will avoid developing a pattern of sexual promiscuity that may be hard to break once you are married. Often, the habits you establish before marriage will become the ones you live by after marriage. Sociologists have discovered that those teenagers who tended to be promiscuous during their teenage years also tend to be promiscuous once they are married. Simply stated, old habits are hard to break.

(10) By avoiding premarital sex, you are more likely to appreciate sex when you experience it in marriage. Generally speaking, the longer you have to wait for something, the more you appreciate it and enjoy it. If you reserve sex for marriage, you will daily reap the emotional rewards that come with a mature decision to preserve sex for your future marriage.

[2]It is interesting to note that the mass media, which often have a liberal view of sex, do not consistently portray the need for safe sex. Nor do the mass media reveal the loneliness and horrors of dying from a sexually transmitted disease. Furthermore, the mass media do not portray the dead-end life of those women trapped in prostitution and pornography. **Lastly, the mass media neither promote the means whereby safe sex may be obtained nor broadcast the benefits of sexual purity.** Obviously, the mass media are not concerned about your safety and security but rather about making money by

showing programs that appeal to the masses. The number one concern of the mass media is that of making money.

[3]By avoiding premarital sex you also will have more time to gain the biblical wisdom necessary to build productive relationships with the opposite sex. Wisdom will give you greater insight into the character of those you date. If you rush into a physical relationship, you will greatly lessen the number of life experiences necessary for helping you make the right decisions concerning a life mate. This is why it is wise never to date just one person or become too close to one person when you first start to date. In fact, the more people you date, the greater the likelihood that you will be in a position to make a wise choice concerning your future spouse. However many people you date, the important thing is that you date people who are also seeking after wisdom. You will have few, if any, regrets during your dating years if you keep to this principle of sexual purity. This is an offshoot of the second principle of wisdom, which emphasizes associating with the wise instead of the foolish.

Are we saying that teenagers should spend the majority of their waking time trying to fill their life full of dates with the opposite sex? Absolutely not! Dating should be only a part of your teenage years. And when you date, it is wise to "group date." This means that you never go out alone with a member of the opposite sex. Group dating is when two or three couples go out together. By "group dating" you can find out more about a person's real personality. It is harder for an individual to hide his or her true personality in a group dating setting. Indeed, group dating also helps you learn more about other peoples' personality types. Above all, group dating will lessen the likelihood of becoming physically involved with another teenager. Group dating reduces the likelihood for intimate encounters and their negative consequences. Thus, group dating has many benefits, the greatest being that it safeguards against premarital sex.

Always remember that as a teenager you have a lot of important areas that need to be addressed. These areas such things as your relationships with your parents and siblings, your schoolwork, school clubs, sports, hobbies, and developing your latent talents for your future employment. To become overly focused on the opposite sex is to create an imbalance in your life. Your overall focus as a teenager is to develop a wise and balanced lifestyle through the use of wisdom, thus increasing the likelihood that you will be happy and healthy both now and in the future.

As a teenager, wisdom encourages you to *gradually* increase your interaction with the opposite sex. A sexual relationship takes a great deal of emotional maturity and commitment, which teenagers have not fully developed. This maturity comes with time and experience. The important point to remember is that dating takes patience and wisdom. The more time you allow yourself for learning about how the opposite sex thinks and acts, the more you will be in a position to make a wise decision regarding your future choice of a marriage partner. This principle of sexual purity will protect you from making decisions that you would later regret. The more wisdom you gain related to the proper place of sex, the greater will be your satisfaction or joy in your future marriage. **Remember, you will never regret keeping yourself sexually pure and saving yourself for marriage.**

Pillar 4

Diligence at Work

"Lazy hands make a man poor, but diligent
hands bring wealth."
(Proverbs 10:4)

Given the fact that you spend a good amount of your waking time either at school or work, it is not surprising that the book of Proverbs has a great deal to say about how you approach your daily responsibilities. Indeed, work plays a significant role in everybody's life. According to the biblical account, one of the first responsibilities God gave to Adam and Eve was that of taking care of, or working, the Garden of Eden.

"The Lord God took the man and put him in the garden
to work it and take care of it." (Genesis 2:15)

Thus, work has been with us from the beginning of time. For the teenager, work usually takes the form of responsibilities at school and at home. Learning to diligently manage these responsibilities can mean the difference between success and failure in life. Hence, the book of Proverbs is remarkably direct concerning the attitudes and actions necessary to effectively manage your daily responsibilities. If there is one overriding word used to describe our responsibility toward our work, that word is *diligence*. Look again at Proverbs 10:4.

> **"Lazy hands make a man poor, but diligent hands bring wealth."**

The word "diligent" in the above verse is a translation of the Hebrew word *charuts*. *Charuts* means "to act promptly or in a decisive manner." In the context of one's responsibilities, *charuts*, or diligence, means that you act promptly to address a job or task. In other words, you address your responsibilities *without hesitation or excuse*. To act in a diligent manner means that you focus all of your knowledge and skills toward your duties in a straightforward manner. Diligence is the opposite of laziness.

Diligence can be viewed as a threefold process. This first step refers to **acquiring the knowledge** necessary to successfully complete a job. As a teenager, this involves making the most of your educational experiences. Be the best possible student you can be. Learn as much as you can. Being a good student is a great way to exercise your mind, ensuring the development of its potential. The greater your education, the greater will be your ability to be diligent in a particular job later in life.

The second step in diligence is **attaining the skills** necessary to address a task. After you have acquired the knowledge necessary to do a job, then you work at developing the actual skills that are required to complete a given task. Skills refer to the application of knowledge to a particular task. The development of your skills may come through on-the-job training or an apprenticeship program. Sometimes an internship is used to develop the job skills of a teenager. Thus, this dimension of diligence emphasizes the importance of learning from others how to develop and sharpen your skills.

The last basic component of diligence is **acting with initiative**. Initiative refers to promptly addressing a task or job at hand. Once you have the knowledge and skills for a job, then you must apply them, without delay. This is crucial for success. Procrastination is the opposite of initiative. Procrastination means that we always have an excuse for not promptly addressing our responsibilities. Diligence, on the other hand, refers to being enthusiastic when faced with a task or responsibility. Notwithstanding how much knowledge and skill one has, procrastination and laziness will quickly bring failure. To be successful, the teenager must act decisively and with enthusiasm when it comes to his or her responsibilities. One must be diligent to practice the skills one has acquired in order to perfect one's mastery of a job.[1] This last dimension of diligence reflects the need for being proactive. If a job needs to be done, then you should "*just do it.*" Avoid distractions and excuses, and just focus on your work. To procrastinate concerning your responsibilities is to squander your opportunities, waste your skills and time, and ultimately bring ruin.

It also should be mentioned that constructive action (diligence) should be directed toward our relationships. No relationship will flourish if one is not diligent to employ those behaviors that will make it work. A teenager cannot expect to have rewarding relationships if he or she does not work at them. Being lazy with our relationships will result in unsatisfactory relationships. On the other hand, if we do right to others, they will most likely return the favor. Laziness in addressing the needs of our friends, spouses, and family members will produce unsatisfying relationships. Satisfying relationships require work! Diligence in employing constructive or beneficial behaviors in our relationships will make our relationships and our lives significantly more fulfilling.

In conclusion, as a teenager you can expect to experience a multitude of positive outcomes by being diligent at your daily responsibilities. Work gives you the opportunity to develop your natural potential and abilities. Work allows you to develop productive skills for life. Diligence helps you to be productively involved in life, thus avoiding destructive pursuits. By being diligently employed at school responsibilities and your job, you will avoid drug use and gang activities. Diligence protects you from the wastefulness of idleness and heightens your chances for success and prosperity. Work provides a sense of accomplishment, thereby constructively influencing your self-esteem. Work keeps you busy and productive, thereby preventing boredom. Furthermore, work can be viewed as a form of therapy, helping you to move beyond life's disappointments and losses. By being diligent in your responsibilities, you are less likely to worry about those issues of life over which you have no control. Work puts your mind on constructive pursuits. Diligence at school, on your job, and in relationships will not only allow you to experience greater levels of achievement and satisfaction, but also will permit you to more fully enjoy your times of leisure and recreation. This paradox of life is true: work makes our times of recreation more fun.

To further your understanding of the fourth pillar of wisdom—diligence for your responsibilities—answer the following questions.

Questions for Further Research and Application

1. Briefly explain the three steps or elements of "diligence."

_____
_____
_____
_____

2. How does work help you to develop your latent or hidden talents?

_____
_____
_____
_____

3. Explain how having a good attitude facilitates success at work.

_____
_____
_____
_____

4. How does work—for example, schoolwork—help you avoid destructive pursuits such as drugs or gang activities?

_____
_____
_____
_____

5. In what ways will your relationships improve if you diligently work on them?

_____
_____
_____
_____

6. Explain the difference between diligence and procrastination.

_____
_____
_____
_____

7. Proverbs is abundantly clear that there is only one way to success and wealth. Read Proverbs 10:4. In what ways are you going to apply this principle to your life?

_____
_____
_____
_____

8. Diligence not only refers to staying busy at work. Sometimes we busy ourselves on tasks that are not really important. This helps us to feel like we are at least doing something. We fritter away our time on lesser or nonessential activities. However, diligence refers to staying busy on the task or tasks that we need to do most. In other words, we prioritize our tasks according to their importance, working on the most important task first. How can prioritizing your daily tasks help you to focus most of your energies on essential tasks?

9. One thing that often hinders our work at school is chasing fantasies or daydreams. Look at Proverbs 12:11.

> **"He who works his land will have abundant food,
> but he who chases fantasies lacks judgment."**

What are the dangers of daydreaming or chasing fantasies when you have work to do?
_____
_____
_____
_____

10. Which of the following habits will help you become a better student?
- Having a regular time to study every day
- Having a regular place to study
- Using an effective plan of study (SQ3R, for example; see note 1 below)
- Using your spare time to review important schoolwork
- Connecting with other students who are serious about school

How can the above habits help you to exercise diligence at school?
_____
_____
_____
_____

11. Read Proverbs 22:13.

> **"The sluggard says, 'There is a lion outside!' or,
> 'I will be murdered in the streets!'"**

The sluggard, or lazy person, often makes up excuses why he or she does not do work. How can you avoid making excuses for your responsibilities, whether at school, home, or work?

_____
_____
_____
_____

12. Being diligent also involves having a good attitude toward your responsibilities. How does a positive attitude help you complete your responsibilities at school and work?

_____
_____
_____
_____

13. Does complaining on your job, or at school, make your responsibilities seem bigger and harder to complete? Is complaining helpful?

_____
_____
_____
_____

14. Why is it important not to "bad-mouth" your teachers at school, who are trying to help you?

_____
_____
_____
_____

15. Why is it important not to "bad-mouth" your boss at work?

_____
_____
_____
_____

16. How will "bad-mouthing" your teachers or your boss affect your attitude toward school or your job?

_____
_____
_____
_____

17. If your attitude is bad toward your teachers or your boss, will you be more or less likely to give your best? What is the connection between your speech and your attitude?

_____
_____
_____
_____

18. Read Proverbs 17:28.
> **"Even a fool is thought wise if he keeps silent,**
> **and discerning if he holds his tongue."**

If you cannot think of anything good to say about your teachers or boss, then should you say anything at all? How does keeping silent sometimes help you to succeed at school and on your job?

_____
_____
_____
_____

19. How will the use of drugs or alcohol affect your ability to be a diligent student at school?

_____
_____
_____
_____

20. How will the use of drugs or alcohol affect your ability to be a diligent worker on your job?

21. How will diligence at your responsibilities improve your chances for success in life?

In summary, as a young person you have much to gain by being diligent at your daily responsibilities. By being faithful in your everyday duties—whether at home, school, or on the job—you will greatly increase your probability for success. Steady work also tends to keep a person out of trouble. Being diligent will help you apply your energies in productive and rewarding activities. **Diligence is a means of not only safeguarding your character but also of building it up.** Being diligent at your duties is the only way to develop your potential and hidden capabilities. There are no shortcuts!

Moreover, diligence in your schoolwork will result in good grades at school. Good grades also will earn you the respect of your parents and teachers. Your self-esteem will improve. You can become your best and feel your best only by giving your best to your daily duties at school.

Hence, according to wisdom, diligence at one's responsibilities is the path that leads to success in life. Whether at school or at work, diligence will bring about achievement and success. This success will result in greater honor and admiration from those around you. And, as your achievements and personal accomplishments increase, so will your self-esteem and self-satisfaction.

- Review and memorize the key verse for the fourth pillar of wisdom.

"Lazy hands make a man poor, but diligent hands bring wealth." (Proverbs 10:4)

- Weekly study schedule: Every Wednesday review and meditate on the fourth pillar of wisdom. Meditate on it throughout the day, and look for opportunities to put it into practice throughout the week.
- Additional verses in Proverbs on being diligent: 6:4-11; 10:4-5; 12:11, 24; 13:4; 14:23; 18:9; 19:24; 20:4, 13; 22:13; 24:27, 30-34; 26:13-16; 27:18; 28:19; 31:15, 17, 27

***

NOTES

[1] SQ3R is a method of study that helps the student to actively and effectively approach any subject matter. An active method of studying will help you to remember a greater amount of material than a passive method.

SQ3R Study Method:
Scan; Question; Read; Recite; Review
An Active Method of Studying

SCAN: Look at the introduction and summary of each chapter of your textbook. Glance over the headings in the chapter to see the main points that will be developed. This should not take more than a minute or two and will reveal the core ideas around which the chapter is focused. This initial scanning will direct your attention to the main ideas of the chapter.

QUESTION: As you scan each chapter, ask yourself the following central question: "What are the central themes of this chapter?" This will focus your curiosity and so increase your comprehension of the core ideas. Asking this key question will help you to see the essence of a given section. *For best results, write the answers to this question on one piece of paper. Use an outline.*

READ: Read the chapter at a rate that keeps your concentration level high. Reading too fast will cause you to miss important points, whereas reading too slowly will give your mind time to wander. Always read with the question in mind, "What are the central themes of this section?" Any *important additional details* that are connected to the central themes also should be written down and added to your core outline of the chapter.

RECITE: After reading the first section of a chapter, look away from the book and recite aloud the answers to your question. Use your own words and include examples. If you can do this, you know what is in the book; if you can't, glance over the section again. An excellent way to do this reciting from memory is to jot down cue phrases in outline form on a sheet of paper. Make the notes very brief. Always connect your answers to the main theme(s) of the chapter.

Now repeat the QUESTION, READ, AND RECITE steps on each subsequent section. That is, turn the next heading within the chapter into a question. Read to answer that question, and then recite the answer by jotting down cue phrases in your notes. Read this way until the entire lesson is completely read and comprehended.

REVIEW: When the chapter or lesson has thus been completely read, look over your notes to get an overview of the main points and their relationship to one another. Check your memory on the context by reciting the major sub-points under each heading. This checking of memory can be done by covering up the notes and trying to recall the sub-points. *For best results, review by giving yourself a self-test. Write out your answers as if you were giving yourself a practice test.* Review again the next day the same materials. The more you review materials that you have studied, the greater the likelihood that you will be able to recall the material on the date of the test. Remember: you remember most what you review most.

Additional study helps:

Get a good night's sleep. Do not come to exams full of coffee or stimulating pop drinks. If you have daily used SQ3R study techniques, there is no need for anxiety or cramming.

Make a realistic schedule for your time each week. List your commitments in order of priority. *School responsibilities should be high on your list!*

- Spiritual growth
- Family
- School
- Sleeping
- Eating
- Exercising
- Socializing
- Entertainment

REMEMBER! Allow time for recreation and some form of exercise that you enjoy.

Pillar 5

Carefulness in Speech

"He who guards his mouth and his tongue keeps himself from calamity."
(Proverbs 21:23)

Aside from sexual purity, the book of Proverbs has more to say about our speech than any other subject. Speech and communication is a natural part of our lives. Given the fact that communication is something that all teenagers do daily, all could benefit from the guidance and wisdom offered by the book of Proverbs concerning patterns of communication.

Teenagers love to talk. They want to share their thoughts, feelings, and creative ideas. In addition, they love to see the humorous side of life and are eager to share their unique perspective on life.

Teenagers often view life from a very different perspective. Indeed, teenagers often have much to communicate concerning themselves and their world. Their novel perspectives on the issues of life can be both inspiring and refreshing.

Yet, teenagers need to be aware of the dangers that can come from using their speech in an unwise manner. Your speech, if used unwisely, can be devastating. Proverbs states, **"Life and death is in the power of the tongue"** (Proverbs 18:21). Our relationships with our family members and with friends can be severely damaged by speaking without wisdom. Moreover, if used unwisely, a teenager's speech can create enemies that last a lifetime. In this section we will examine the tremendous impact that communication has in the life of a teenager.

To further your understanding of the fifth pillar of wisdom—carefulness in speech—answer the following questions.

Questions for Further Research and Application

1. Wisdom focuses on thoughtful speech. Why is it important to "think" before we speak?

___

2. Read Proverbs 18:13.
> **"He who answers before listening—that is his folly and his shame."**

Why is it important to carefully listen to others before we give them our thoughts?

___

3. Sometimes people (family and friends) say things that irritate us.
"A fool shows his annoyance at once, but a prudent man overlooks an insult." (Proverbs 12:16)

What can happen if we are quick to show our annoyance at another?
_____
_____
_____
_____

4. Read Proverbs 17:14.
"Starting a quarrel is like breaching a dam; so drop the matter before a dispute breaks out."

Should we be quick to show our annoyance and start an argument, or should we try to maintain our composure and just overlook hurtful or annoying comments? Why is it important to avoid being argumentative with others?
_____
_____
_____
_____

5. See Proverbs 15:1:
"A gentle answer turns away wrath, but a harsh word stirs up anger."

If you find yourself already in an argument, then a gentle or soft answer can help to diffuse the heat of the moment. Why is it important to "keep your cool" when a conversation becomes heated?
_____
_____
_____
_____

6. Proverbs has a lot to say about speaking with honesty. Read Proverbs 14:25 and 24:26.

"A truthful witness saves lives, but a false witness is deceitful." (Proverbs 14:25)
"An honest answer is like a kiss on the lips." (Proverbs 24:26)

One person has described dishonesty as being "a slap to one's face!" Why is an honest answer like "a kiss on the lips"?

_____
_____
_____
_____

7. Can friendships grow and develop without honesty? Why is honesty important to any relationship?

_____
_____
_____
_____

8. Being honest is only one side of the coin. For communication to be truly effective, it must also be caring. Consider Proverbs 16:24.
"Pleasant words are a honeycomb, sweet to the soul, healing to the bones."

What does this verse tell us about the importance of using pleasant words when we communicate to others?

_____
_____
_____
_____

9. What often happens when honesty is expressed without kindness? Are you more receptive or less receptive to someone who speaks to you in a harsh and inconsiderate manner? Why?

_____
_____

10. Look at Proverbs 16:21.
   > **"The wise in heart are discerning, and pleasant words promote instruction."**

If you want your friends to listen or learn from you, how should you speak to them?

11. Examine Proverbs 16:28 and 26:20.
   > **"A gossip separates close friends." (Proverbs 16:28)**
   > **"Without wood a fire goes out; without gossip a quarrel dies down." (Proverbs 26:20)**

According to these two proverbs, what are two negative outcomes of gossip?

12. Read Proverbs 22:24-25.
   > **"Do not make friends with a hot-tempered man; do not associate with one easily angered, or you may learn his ways and get yourself ensnared."**

Why is it also important to avoid associating with the talkative and hot-tempered person?

13. Look at Proverbs 10:19.
> **"When words are many, sin is not absent;
> but he who holds his tongue is wise."**

Restraining our speech gives us more time to think about the long-term impact that our speech has on others. This in turn can help keep us out of trouble, especially in avoiding gossip and arguments. How can "holding our tongue" help us to avoid an argument or put a stop to an argument once it has started?

_____
_____
_____
_____

14. Read Proverbs 17:22a.
> **"A cheerful heart is good medicine." (Proverbs 17:22a)**

What are the benefits—both to ourselves and to others—in expressing cheerfulness in our speech?

_____
_____
_____
_____

15. How does constructive or positive speech affect your chances for success at school?

_____
_____
_____
_____

16. How does positive and respectful communication affect your chances for success on your job?

_____
_____
_____
_____

17. Can you have a happy dating relationship or happy marriage without being careful with your speech? Why?
_____
_____
_____
_____

18. How will wise speech affect your chances for satisfaction with your family relationships?
_____
_____
_____
_____

19. Does your speech usually reflect your character?
_____
_____
_____
_____

20. How does your speech affect your reputation with others?
_____
_____
_____
_____

21. In what constructive ways will wise and thoughtful speech enrich your life?
_____
_____
_____
_____
_____
_____

To summarize, your speech will greatly affect all aspects of your life. Your relationships will be significantly impacted by your manner of speech. Your friendships will be either nourished or stressed by your patterns of communication. Your speech, if used wisely, will draw both your family and friends closer to you. Wisdom encourages us to speak less and with greater thoughtfulness for others. Furthermore, by speaking with wisdom, your chances for success at school and on your job will multiply. Wisdom in speech is necessary for obtaining satisfying relationships. *Wise speech produces greater peace and harmony both at home and at work.* In the end, wise speech not only increases the likelihood for success but also brings about greater personal happiness.

- Review and memorize the key verse for the fifth pillar of wisdom.

"He who guards his mouth and his tongue keeps himself from calamity." (Proverbs 21:23)

- Weekly study schedule: Every Thursday review and meditate on the fifth pillar of wisdom. Meditate on it throughout the day, and look for opportunities to put it into practice throughout the week.
- Additional verses in Proverbs on being careful in speech: 6:2-3; 10:18-20; 11:13; 12:16; 13:2-3; 14:29; 15:1-2, 18, 28; 16:21, 24, 32; 17:7, 9; 18:2, 4, 6-7, 13, 19-21; 19:11; 20:15; 29:5, 8-11, 20, 22.

Pillar 6

Simplicity of Lifestyle

"Do not wear yourself out to get rich, have
the wisdom to show restraint."
(Proverbs 23:4)

One of the more common fantasies of teenagers is that of acquiring money or wealth. Indeed, many teenagers will freely admit that greed is just a normal part of their lives. They see many adults in our society chasing after a lifestyle of greed. Moreover, to further influence the thinking of teenagers, the mass media (especially television) are always setting forth the latest fad that teenagers "need" to have in order to be cool or be accepted by their peers. The mass media, by means of commercials and popular movies, tries to manipulate the minds of teenagers to buy into a materialistic mind-set. But what are the consequences of a materialistic and greedy mind-set?

Many teenagers often think that if they have enough money to buy more things, they might finally achieve personal satisfaction. Indeed, both teenagers and adults tend to fall prey to the pitfalls of greed and materialism. "If only I had more and more money, I could buy such and such—more and more stuff!" "Then everybody will like me, love me, or accept me." But is this the way of wisdom? *Will "more money" and "more things" really make you happy?* Will buying the latest fad or designer clothing make you popular, or will others simply become jealous and envious of you? Let's take a closer look at greed and the accumulation of wealth as it affects your personal happiness.

To further your understanding of the sixth pillar of wisdom—simplicity of lifestyle—answer the following questions.

Questions for Further Research and Application

1. How does simplicity of lifestyle relate to your personal happiness? In other words, how does living a simple life contribute to happiness? Why?

_____
_____
_____
_____

2. Does having more "things" make life easier or more complicated?

_____
_____
_____
_____

3. One astute teenager has said that the more you have, the more you have to take care of! In other words, the more things you have, the more responsibilities you have. More and more responsibilities bring on greater stress. Read **Ecclesiastes 4:6:**

"Better one handful with tranquility than two handfuls with toil and chasing after the wind."

What does it mean to you to have "one handful with tranquility"? How does this proverb affect your attitude toward the accumulation of things?

_____
_____
_____
_____

4. What is the difference between buying at the best-known, expensive department stores and buying from discount stores?

_____
_____
_____
_____

5. Do you really need clothes that have a foreign or exotic name attached to them? Does the "designer name" somehow make you a better person? Why or why not?

_____
_____
_____
_____

6. Some teenagers buy the "latest" clothes so they will fit in with the "in group." What is the danger of this type of thinking?

_____
_____
_____
_____

7. Do you really need to buy things that are new? For example, could a good used car adequately serve your transportation needs instead of a new car?

8. From a non-materialistic perspective, do you really need more money or more things to be truly happy?

9. From the viewpoint of wisdom, what gives real meaning to our lives?

10. Sometimes the desire for getting rich quickly (greed) leads to gambling. This can be a real temptation for a teenager. Gambling, more often than not, leads to the loss of your money. Gambling—whether at casinos or on the internet or in the stock market—eventually leads to financial loss or ruin. Taking into account what the fourth pillar of wisdom (Diligence at Work) has to say about earning your money through honest work, what should be a teenager's attitude concerning any form of gambling? What are some forms of gambling a teenager may be tempted to get involved with?

11. As in the case of gambling, can a young person really appreciate money that has been acquired without any real work involved? See Proverbs 10:2 and 13:11.

"Ill-gotten treasures are of no value." (Proverbs 10:2)

"Dishonest money dwindles away, but he who gathers money little by little makes it grow." (Proverbs 13:11)

What usually happens to money quickly gained through gambling or other "get-rich-quick" schemes?
_____
_____
_____
_____

12. Note that Proverbs 13:11 tells us that by saving money "little by little" we can make it grow. How does this verse speak to you as a teenager?
_____
_____
_____
_____

13. Does greed promote dishonesty? How can greed encourage theft from one's employer?
_____
_____
_____
_____

14. How does embracing a life of simplicity help you to live with greater honesty and integrity?
_____
_____
_____
_____

15. How does living a life of simplicity promote greater peace of mind and personal contentment?
_____
_____

16. See Proverbs 1:11-15
"**If they say, 'come along with us; let's lie in wait for someone's blood, let's waylay some harmless soul; let us swallow them alive, like the grave, and whole, like those who go down to the pit;** *we will get all sorts of valuable things and fill our house with plunder.* **Throw in your lot with us and we will share a common purse.' My son do not go along with them.**"

Does greed (love for money or material things) also make a teenager more susceptible to committing harm to another? What other crimes might a teenager commit because of greed?

_____
_____
_____
_____

17. Look again at the above verses in question 16. What is King Solomon's counsel to teenagers when it comes to joining a gang in order to get "all sorts of valuable things"?

_____
_____
_____
_____

18. In connection with this chapter's focus on the avoidance of greed and the embracing of simplicity, what does the following statement mean to you? "When your output exceeds your intake, then your upkeep becomes your downfall."

_____
_____
_____
_____

19. How does greed affect our relationships with others? Does greed make us less or more generous toward others?

20. Look at Proverbs 15:27, **"A greedy man brings trouble to his family."** Also, Proverbs 15:17 says, **"Better a meal of vegetables where there is love, than a fattened calf with hatred."** Which family is likely to be more happy and content—the family that has an "attitude of gratitude" for the simple pleasures of life and for their simple meals, or the family that has much but is always desiring more and more?

21. In what constructive ways will a simple and greedless lifestyle improve your life?

In conclusion, greed is a normal part of our society—even among teenagers. Yet, the wise teenager understands that having more money or things is not the route to personal satisfaction. The route to personal satisfaction comes from having fulfilling relationships with our family and friends. Also, diligence at work adds to one's level of fulfillment. Simplicity of lifestyle allows you to greatly appreciate and rejoice in the simple pleasures of life. A lifestyle of simplicity and an attitude of gratitude go hand in hand. Simplicity of lifestyle allows you to love God with greater devotion, and without the distractions of material pursuits. Furthermore, a lifestyle of simplicity helps to guard you from engaging in foolish activities like gambling or investing in the stock market. Greed promotes deception, dishonesty, and criminal activities. Just as simplicity and honesty go hand in hand, so also does greed and dishonesty go together. Simplicity of living helps you to live and work with greater integrity and honesty. In the end, the more uncomplicated and unpretentious your lifestyle, the greater the likelihood for personal integrity and contentment.

- Review and memorize the key verse for the sixth pillar of wisdom.

    "Do not wear yourself out to get rich, have the wisdom to show restraint." (Proverbs 23:4)

- Weekly study schedule: Every Friday review and meditate on the sixth pillar of wisdom. Meditate on it throughout the day, and look for opportunities to put it into practice throughout the week.
- Additional verses in Proverbs on simplicity of lifestyle: 3:9-10; 11:16, 28; 13:7-8, 11; 15:15-17, 27; 16:8; 17:1; 18:23; 21:17; 22:1, 7b; 23:1-5, 20, 21; 28:6, 11, 20, 22, 25; 30:7 –9.

Pillar 7

Compassion for the Less Fortunate

"He who is kind to the poor lends to the Lord,
and he will be rewarded for what he has done."
(Proverbs 19:17)

As we have seen already, God does bring wealth to those who are diligent in their responsibilities. Yes, even as a teenager, your diligence at work will bring wealth your way. Yet, besides taking care of our needs, what is the real purpose for having money? Is it only for the accumulation of things? Is wealth to be used to buy more and more toys in order to make ourselves the center of attention and our friends envious of us? Or is there a higher purpose when one reaps the abundant blessings of wisdom?

Teenagers today are often tempted to focus on material pursuits alone. There is an abundance of TV commercials selling a materialistic way of life. On the other hand, there are not any TV commercials that I am aware of that tell teenagers to look above the material things in life. Most, if not all, commercials for teenagers focus on the latest fashion or "craze." Teenagers are constantly bombarded with commercials urging them to live solely for themselves, or to buy the "coolest" clothes, or to get the latest technology toy. Yet, the wise teenager will ask if any of these things will lead to personal fulfillment. Is the chase for materialism and more "things" the way to a meaningful existence in your life? Or does wisdom point to a different use of our prosperity and wealth? The following questions will help you to gain a unique and prudent perspective on wealth and its uses.

To further your understanding of the seventh pillar of wisdom—compassion for the less fortunate—answer the following questions.

Questions for Further Research and Application

1. Look at Proverbs 11:25.
   "A generous person will prosper; he who refreshes others will himself be refreshed."

According to this proverb, what is the outcome for those who refresh or help others?

_____
_____
_____
_____

2. Look at Proverbs 19:17: **"He who is kind to the poor lends to the Lord, and he will be rewarded for what he has done."** This is the only verse in the Bible that describes God in terms of becoming a borrower to a human. What an awesome thought! According to this verse, God becomes obligated to anyone who is "kind to the poor." As a teenager, how does this verse impress on you the importance that God places on helping the poor and the less fortunate?

_____
_____

3. What are some of the ways you can be kind to the poor?

4. How can volunteering your time for others be beneficial to you as well as to others?

5. What are some ways you can help the needy or elderly within your own family?

6. By being generous to others, we can also inherit a promise. Look again at Proverbs 11:25.
> **"A generous man will prosper; he who refreshes others will himself be refreshed." (Proverbs 11:25)**

What promise does this proverb hold out for any teenager? What does it mean to you to be "refreshed"?

7. Are there any community service projects that you could be involved in that provide services to the poor or disadvantaged? Name at least two.

_____
_____
_____
_____

8. What activities could you participate in with your family or friends that would be beneficial to the underprivileged?

_____
_____
_____
_____

9. What activities at your church could you join to benefit the poor?

_____
_____
_____
_____

10. In the book of Proverbs, God is viewed as having a special place in His heart for the destitute, especially the poor and abandoned. Read Proverbs 22:22-23.

> **"Do not exploit the poor because they are poor, and do not crush the needy in court. For the Lord will take up their case and will plunder those who plunder them."**

What do these two verses mean to you?

_____
_____
_____
_____

11. Read the following proverb.
> **"He who oppresses the poor shows contempt for his Maker, but whoever is kind to the needy honors God." (Proverbs 14:31)**

How does one honor God by being kind to the needy?
_____
_____
_____
_____

12. Being a giving or loving person is a key attribute of wisdom. Look at the following proverb.
> **"He who pursues righteousness and love finds life, prosperity and honor." (Proverbs 21:21)**

According to this verse, what are the outcomes of pursuing compassion for the needy?
_____
_____
_____
_____

13. How does the Golden Rule ("Do unto others as you would have them do unto you") overlap with the principle of compassion for the less fortunate?
_____
_____
_____
_____

14. Read Proverbs 11:16-17.
> **"A kindhearted person gains respect, but ruthless men gain only wealth."**
> **"A kind man benefits himself, but a cruel man brings himself to harm."**

In what ways can you show kindness to other teenagers?
_____
_____
_____

15. The following list identifies some ways you can share compassion with others.
    - Working at or visiting an orphanage
    - Working with an organization for unwed mothers
    - Working with the homeless through a homeless shelter
    - Visiting the sick, or "homebound"—especially the elderly
    - Visiting and helping widows or the disabled who are part of your church

In which of these areas would you be most interested in working?
_____
_____
_____

16. If the above areas seem a little too big to start with, then start in your own neighborhood. There is always someone within every neighborhood that is in need of help—someone who has just experienced a traumatic accident or disease. Start working with one person at a time, and schedule visits. Working with the elderly or sickly in your neighborhood is a great way to help the less fortunate. You will be amazed at how this will make you feel. Instead of watching TV or going to the movies, take some time to be helpful to the elderly or shut-ins. How will helping or serving such people make them feel?
_____
_____
_____

17. How would you feel if you were a "shut-in" and a teenager offered his or her help to you?

18. What fundraisers at school could you be involved in as a means of helping the needy?

19. At school there are usually kids who are poor, handicapped, or "socially lacking." These students are sometimes "left out" by the other students. How would befriending them help them feel better about themselves?

20. How does showing compassion to the less fortunate help to bring us back to the first pillar of wisdom (humility)?

21. In what constructive ways would kindness for the less fortunate enrich your life?

As a teenager it is all too easy to neglect the less fortunate. Too often we are focused only on our own needs and problems. The mass media portrays teenagers as egocentric and focused purely on their own lives. Yet, for those teens who have embraced this pillar of wisdom—service to others—their levels of personal satisfaction have significantly risen. They have discovered how rewarding it is when they allow their lives to be touched by those who are in need.

Some of the greatest treasures in life are experienced by means of interacting with and assisting the needy. Helping others is what gives true meaning to our lives. A smile, a listening ear, a word of encouragement, a helping hand, an unsolicited or anonymous gift, a patient attitude—these acts of kindness can be used anytime, whether in a store checkout, in congested traffic, in our neighborhood, or with our own family members! Through patience and compassion, we strengthen our ties and connection with our fellow human beings. We reconnect with the fact that we are all part of the family of humanity. In realizing this last principle of wisdom, we bring ourselves back full circle to the first pillar of wisdom, the principle of humility. It takes humility to help those in need, but in so doing you will reap the honor of being a true lover of humanity.

- Review and memorize the key verse for the seventh pillar of wisdom.

"He who is kind to the poor lends to the Lord, and he will be rewarded for what he has done."
(Proverbs 19:17)

- Every Saturday review and meditate on the seventh pillar of wisdom. Meditate on it throughout the day, and look for opportunities to put it into practice throughout the week.
- Additional verses in Proverbs on love for the less fortunate: 3:3-4, 27-28; 11:16-17, 24-25, 30; 14:21, 31; 17:5; 19:17, 22; 21:13; 22:9, 16, 22-23; 24:11; 28:8, 22, 27; 29:7, 14; 31:8, 9, 20.

Concluding Statement

In closing, we must be careful to remember that everyday we are faced with many important choices. The choices we make, over time, will determine our character. And, ultimately, our character will determine our destiny. Whether our destinies are filled with hope, prosperity, and peace or are filled with despair, poverty, and regret will depend to a vast extent on the degree to which we choose to accept or ignore the Seven Pillars of Wisdom.

APPENDICES

Section I: Helpful Outlines

Appendix A:
Living with Greater Humility

The following brief outline is designed to help teenagers live each day with greater humility.

Seven directives for cultivating greater humility in your life

1. Be respectful to all people of all ages and all nationalities. (Smile and greet all as part of your extended family)

2. Be thankful for the simple wonders in nature and life.

3. Be grateful for all the individuals who have helped you in your past and present.

4. Work hard as a means to success. (Do not look for the easy or quick way to success.)

5. Be less talkative and more thoughtful of others (especially of their feelings and thoughts).

6. Be simple in your lifestyle, seeking to use less of the earth's limited natural resources.

7. Be compassionate and helpful to those who are weak, poor, disabled, or less fortunate.

Appendix B:
Living with Greater Carefulness in Companionship

The following brief outline is designed to help teenagers obtain wise friendships.

Seven dimensions for wisely choosing your friends and associates

1. Choose friends who are *humble in their attitudes* (vs. prideful attitudes).

2. Choose friends who are *cautious in their friendships* (vs. foolish friends).

3. Choose friends who *strive for sexual purity*; your friends should embrace abstinence if they are unmarried, or sexual loyalty if they are married (vs. loose morals).

4. Choose friends who are *diligent at their responsibilities* at home, school, and work (vs. laziness or using drugs).

5. Choose friends who are *careful in their speech* (vs. thoughtless speech).

6. Choose friends who are *simple in their lifestyles*. (vs. extravagant life styles)

7. Choose friends who are *compassionate toward others* (vs. apathetic attitudes and actions toward the less fortunate).

In summary, Finding the right associates in life is fundamentally a matter of choosing individuals who exhibit the seven core qualities of wisdom.

Appendix C:
Living with Greater Sexual Purity

The following brief outline is designed to help teenagers maintain sexual purity.

Seven directives for sexual purity

1. *Keep your focus as a teenager on getting an education.* This includes an education about wisdom, as well as an education in traditional subjects. The more you learn, the farther you will go in life and the higher will be your self-esteem. By focusing on your education, you will greatly increase your chances for getting the career of your choice. (Your education, including your knowledge of wisdom, will be the chief means of achieving success at your future career.)

2. *Connect up with friends who favor sexual purity or sexual abstinence.* There are some people who look upon sex as just an appetite to be fulfilled. The wise consider sex to be a symbol of a deep commitment between two people. Connect up with people who view sex as part of a deeper, life-long commitment.

3. *Avoid dating people who have no clear understanding of the benefits of sexual purity.* People who understand the tremendous advantages of sexual purity are more motivated to save themselves for marriage.

4. *Be aware of, and meditate on, the significant rewards of sexual purity.* This will help you to be more motivated to refrain from pre-marital sex.

5. *Be aware of, and meditate on, the significant negative consequences of premarital sex.* This will significantly add to your motivation for avoiding pre-marital sex.

6. *Avoid looking at immodestly dressed women/men or pornography.* Looking at either incites lusts and promotes a "live-only-for-today" attitude. This type of attitude will not bring about success in life or lasting satisfaction in your relationships. Moreover, the time stolen by pornography keeps you from working on and obtaining your educational and life goals.[1]

7. *Engage in extracurricular activities that will invigorate and strengthen you.* These include activities like sports, hobbies, exercise, music, and the arts. These activities will help to "balance" your life and will make you a more interesting and "well-rounded" individual.

***

NOTES

[1] To sum up the destructive nature of pornography: Looking at pornography not only encourages sexual impurity and infidelity, but it also has other negative results. Pornography, at the very least, can result in a tremendous waste of time. Young people who look at pornography neglect more important responsibilities in their lives. Anyone who spends hours looking at pornography obviously will have less time to work on responsibilities at home, school, and work. Pornography can consume time that could be used doing enjoyable things together with good friends or with your family. Pornography keeps you from using your time to help others. The bottom line is that the more time you spend on pornography, the less time you have for developing yourself in a balanced manner. Pornography takes away from the time you would otherwise use to build satisfying relationships. In the end, pornography not only gives one a false and imbalanced view of sex, but it also keeps you from being all that you could be.

Appendix D:
Living with Greater Diligence in Your Work

The following brief outline is designed to help teenagers be diligent at their daily responsibilities.

Seven directives for diligence

1. *Get as much education as possible.* Getting an education in the field of wisdom is the first priority. This will help you make the most of your opportunities at school. Then study to gain more knowledge in your chosen career field. Even after you have obtained the job of your choice, continue to engage in professional development. This helps you to stay updated concerning recent advancements in your field.

2. *At the beginning of each day, make a "to-do" list of tasks that need to be completed.* First, make a list of your responsibilities. Making this list focuses your attention for the day. Second, prioritize your list according to importance. Number your tasks with the most important task being #1, the second most important task being #2, and so forth. At school, this means working on the most important subjects first. At home, this means doing your chores before you play or relax.

3. *Work the "prioritized" list enthusiastically.* Start with the top priority on your list and work on it with undivided attention and energy. By working with enthusiasm, you build momentum. Momentum is a positive force that will help you to complete your tasks promptly. This dimension of wisdom will allow you to be an achiever instead of a dreamer.

4. *Focus on having a positive attitude concerning your responsibilities, whether at school or work.* Focus on the benefits of getting a good education. Avoid negative thoughts and speech concerning your teachers or your work. Negative thoughts and speech

will only generate a negative attitude, and this will create a mental drag, making the job harder. A positive attitude will give you a head start on your work. Having a positive attitude at work also will bring about positive outcomes.

5. *Get to school or work EARLY everyday.* Getting to school or work a few minutes early each day will help you to build positive momentum for the day, and it will give you a head start on your work. It will give you a few extra minutes to review your work. Getting to school early also will make a positive impression on your teacher! Likewise, getting to work early will impress your boss and help you to build momentum for your responsibilities.

6. *Be a team player, whether at school, on the job.* Being a team player helps you to increase your productivity and enhances your relationships. When you are a team player, you create synergism, which helps everyone to finish a job promptly. Teamwork divides the effort and multiplies the effect (outcomes). Compliment others for their successes. Play off of your teammates' strengths. Celebrate their accomplishments. Being a team player eventually will come back to you in the form of both positive relationships and greater achievements.

7. *Treat your body with respect.* Your mind and your body must be taken care of in order for you to be productive in life. Wisdom will protect your mind. When it comes to your body, be sure to get plenty of rest and eat foods that are good for you. Avoid gluttony and drugs. Engage in healthy lifestyle practices such as exercise in order to maximize your energy levels and mental abilities. To sum up: aim for adequate levels of sleep, good food, exercise, and the avoidance of drugs. A healthy body is necessary in order to have the energy to be an effective and productive student and worker.

Appendix E:
Living with Greater Control of Your Speech

The following brief outline is designed to help teenagers exercise greater wisdom in their daily communication with others.

Seven directives for speaking with wisdom

1. ***Let your speech be governed by thoughtfulness.*** Stop and think: "Is this the right time and place for what I am about to say?" If you are not sure that it is the right time or place, then do not say it. In other words, be thoughtful before you speak. Being patient and thoughtful before you say something is the first step in using wisdom concerning your speech. Those who are thoughtful in their speech tend to be less regretful of what they say to others.

2. ***Show empathy***. Learn to actively listen to others and communicate back to them what they are feeling and thinking. This is a great way to make and keep friends. It is also a great way to avoid making enemies. Strive to understand others first. Then offer to share your feelings and thoughts, but do not force your opinions on another. Speaking with empathy is at the heart of compassionate communication. Listen and reflect on what others are saying. Speaking with empathy is especially effective when helping those who are experiencing loss or great challenges in their lives. Sometimes the only thing another person needs is having someone who will genuinely and carefully listen!

3. ***Be honest***. Telling the truth is still the best policy. Honesty is a rare element that is missing in modern communication. But it is the foundation upon which relationships are built. However, in order for honesty to be productive it must be used with the other directives of speech! Honesty must be balanced with empathy (#2) and a non-judgmental attitude (#4) in order for it to be effective.

4. *Be nonjudgmental*. Avoid being condemning or offensive in your speech. Being judgmental never brings about mutually fulfilling relationships. The more accepting you can be of others, the more likely it is they will listen to you. You can be judgmental (analytical) of another's thinking and behavior without being critical of the person.

5. *Be encouraging*. An important aspect of wise speech is encouragement. Thus, one's speech should be used for the support of others, especially your family and friends. Encouragement includes communicating with others your belief in their ability to persevere and succeed when facing life challenges.

6. *Express appreciation*. Another important dimension of wise speech is telling others how much you value them. This includes your family members and friends who have helped you. Actively look for opportunities to show gratitude. Gratitude should be expressed not just for the big helps that we receive from others but also for the little ones. You will be amazed at how this will improve your outlook on life. Also use your speech to express recognition and appreciation for the simple pleasures of everyday life. Appreciation for others and the simple pleasures of life is an important part of both optimism and interpersonal attraction. Apathy, complaining, and cynicism tend to drive others away. Moreover, these types of negative speech tend to bring on depression.

7. *Be instructive*. Be willing to share with others the wisdom and knowledge that has been helpful to you. As you grow in wisdom, and as you start to experience its rewards, you will find that there are many who are seeking better strategies to manage their lives. Sharing wisdom with others is at the heart of helping those in need. Wisdom was designed for helping others. Wisdom can improve anyone's quality of life. In the end, sharing wisdom is beneficial both to you and to your listener.

Appendix F:
Living with Greater Simplicity of Lifestyle

The following brief outline is designed to help teenagers live with greater simplicity.

Seven directives for living with greater simplicity

1. *Avoid gluttony.* Eating is something we do often during the day. Learning to manage your eating habits is an important part of learning to manage yourself. Eat foods in moderation, and move toward meals that include whole gains, vegetables, and fruits. Eat principally for health and secondarily for the pleasure of taste. The wise consider eating, while pleasurable, to be a sacred act.

2. *Avoid greed.* The love of money increases one's likelihood for criminal acts, such as robbery and even murder. Likewise, the desire for more things or stuff also promotes unwise actions or behaviors. Greed promotes interpersonal conflicts. On the other hand, simplicity of lifestyle decreases the likelihood for acts of crime such as theft, robbery, or murder. The person who avoids greed experiences higher levels of inner peace and more satisfying relationships.

3. *Embrace the simple over the extravagant or exotic.* This is especially helpful in the areas of food and material items. (For example, a simple, healthy meal is easier to fix than an exotic meal. And a simple meal is usually better for you. Likewise, a smaller house is easier to take care of than a large house. And a good, used car is more practical than a "muscle" car or an expensive prestige car.

4. *Keep to a regular, simple sleeping pattern.* As Benjamin Franklin said, "Early to bed and early to rise makes one healthy, wealthy, and wise." A regular, early bedtime pattern will maximize energy returns. This will help you to be more productive at school, home, and at work. Furthermore, an early sleeping pattern tends

to allow one to think more clearly during the day. You will not be walking around during the day in a "mental fog." Moreover, by getting to bed early, you will avoid the late-night party scene, where alcohol, gluttony, and promiscuity tend to be more prevalent.

5. *Adopt clothing that is simple.* Choose standard clothes over "designer" and/or flashy clothes. This helps to avoid ego expansion. An easy way to exercise more humility is to purposely dress with plain clothes, especially clothes that are not associated with a designer's name or a company that is highly esteemed by the media. Clothes should not be a means of drawing attention to ourselves but simply a means for protecting us from the elements and providing comfort. Avoid clothes that are too loose, too bright, or too tight. Extreme clothing tends to draw undue attention to the wearer. Humility is paramount.

6. *Use daily prayer.* Both prayer and meditation on God's Word helps us to connect to a higher power and a greater source of wisdom. Prayer helps us to remain humble by reminding us that we are not the center of the universe but only a small part of it. Prayer also helps us to connect to someone much bigger than ourselves—the Creator of the universe—God. The wonderful thing about prayer is that it can be engaged in anytime during the day. It helps us to live a simpler life by taking the focus off of ourselves and our materialistic pursuits. Effective prayer moves us away from an ego-centered position and helps us to be more involved with God and others. Through prayer we can remain centered on the most important things in life, especially our relationships with others and God. Ultimately, prayer will bring significantly more peace and personal satisfaction to our daily lives.

For greater simplicity in your life, start a collection of prayers that you can use throughout your day. This will facilitate a regular prayer life. Start a prayer journal in which you record your journey into greater prayerfulness. A great prayer to start with is the "serenity prayer.[1] *Spurgeon's Sermons on Great Prayers of the Bible* is a fantastic collection of biblical prayers and the blessings they hold for us.

7. ***Choose wise friends.*** As noted in the second pillar of wisdom, your friends will have a tremendous impact on your attitudes and your actions. Look for friends who cherish and try to live a life of simplicity. A friend who chooses to live a simple and non-materialistic life is a true treasure. This in turn helps you to value the simple pleasures of life. Wise and simple friends are hard to find, but they are worth the search.

***

NOTES

[1]God grant me the serenity
to accept the things I cannot change,
courage to change the things I can,
and wisdom to know the difference.
(St. Francis of Assisi)

Appendix G:
Living with Greater Love for the Less Fortunate

The following brief outline is designed to help teenagers help those in need.

Seven directives for greater love

1. *Adopt an inclusive attitude concerning the human race.* View the human race as being one immense, yet diverse family. This attitude will help to maximize mutual peace and goodwill. An inclusive attitude stresses cooperation. By embracing an attitude that we are essentially one big family, you are promoting greater peace on earth. Thus, all teenagers are to be viewed as your brothers and sisters.

2. *Live simply*. This directive is a throwback to wisdom principle #6, Simplicity of Lifestyle. By living simply, you will have more time to focus on the rewarding work of helping others. Those who choose to live extravagantly tend to have little time for those who are in need. They are too busy trying to collect "stuff" or taking care of all of the "stuff" they have accumulated. A simple lifestyle is easier to manage and is therefore less demanding and less stressing. Moreover, an unpretentious lifestyle will help you to get your mind off of yourself, allowing more time to be involved with others and their needs.

3. *Help someone within your family*. Look for those most in need in your family or extended family. Start by listening and being empathetic. Then be willing to "get your hands dirty" and get involved. Helping someone within your own family is the first step toward making your world a better place. It is a great place to learn how to be of assistance. The family is the basic building block of all societies. By showing compassion within your family, you are strengthening not only your family but also society as a whole.

4. Help at least one person in your neighborhood or community. After your own family, seek out someone in need from your neighborhood. This may involve the handicapped or the elderly. The handicapped and the elderly provide for us great opportunities to help—from picking up groceries or doing yard work or just being with them. Sometimes those in need just desire someone to listen to them. The elderly offer a wealth of experience and wisdom.

5. Keep a positive attitude when it comes to another's ability to change. Have faith in people. Maintain and express an unshakable faith in the ability of others to change for the better. Keep your attitude positive concerning the ability of others to change, notwithstanding how many time they have fail. In other words, avoid a cynical attitude concerning humankind. The human potential for self-actualization is amazing.

6. Join a community-based team or program for helping. By being part of a team, you will be more effective in helping the less fortunate. Join a program that is being offered through your church, school, or other community organization. Connecting with others who are "doing good" will help create a sense of mutual support and encouragement. Being a part of a team creates synergism—greater power to do greater good. Thus, being part of a team will multiple your efforts for doing good.

7. Treat all with respect, especially the poor and destitute. Wherever you go or whatever you do, commit yourself to showing respect and treating all people with kindness and fairness. This brings us back to the first directive of viewing all people as being part of the same family. If we are all part of the same family, we should be willing to show respect to all. By doing this, you are not only demonstrating humility but also helping to make the world a better place, a place with greater peace for all.

Section II
Supplemental Information

Appendix H:
12 Specific Benefits of Wisdom

"Happy, blessed, and fortunate is the man who finds wisdom" (Proverbs 3:13)

Why are people "happy, blessed, and fortunate" when they embrace wisdom? This section will answer that question by identifying some of the specific benefits of wisdom. By realizing the many specific rewards that come from wisdom, the teenager will quickly comprehended wisdom's true value. More importantly, by recognizing the specific rewards connected to wisdom, the teenager is motivated to invest the necessary time and energy into fully embracing wisdom.

These specific rewards show how wisdom will impact the individual's life daily in a constructive, practical way. Thus, the following statements point out ***definite physical, emotional, career, and spiritual rewards*** that will be gained from choosing wisdom.

1. Wisdom brings peace: Proverbs 3:17.
2. Wisdom bestows love: Proverbs 8:17.
3. Wisdom brings long life: Proverbs 4:10; 13:14.
4. Wisdom gives riches and wealth: Proverbs 8:18.
5. Wisdom grants honor and respect: Proverbs 4:8.
6. Wisdom brings healing and health: Proverbs 4: 20-22.
7. Wisdom gives us stamina and strength: Proverbs 4:12.
8. Wisdom provides deep and restful sleep: Proverbs 3:24.
9. Wisdom provides safety and freedom from fear: Proverbs 1:33.
10. Wisdom provides us with a bright hope for our futures: Proverbs 24:14.
11. Wisdom protects us from foolish behavior and foolish people: Proverbs 2:11-15.
12. Wisdom gives us the knowledge to build a happy and secure family: Proverbs 24:3.

Truly, there is a wealth of benefits to be gain from walking according to the seven pillars of wisdom!

Appendix I:
A Simple Weekly Schedule for Obtaining Greater Wisdom

Interestingly, just as there are seven pillars of wisdom, there are also seven days of the week. To help make wisdom a greater part of your life, assign one day of the week for each pillar/principle of wisdom. Then meditate on verses from the book of Proverbs that correspond to that pillar of wisdom. By studying and meditating on a particular principle of wisdom on a set day of the week, you are more likely to incorporate wisdom into your daily thinking. This in turn will increase the chances for choosing a more successful and satisfying way of living. Walking in greater wisdom is a *daily choice*.

For example, here is a simple schedule that helps to make each pillar of wisdom a part of your daily life

1. Sunday: Humility: The Supreme Attitude
2. Monday: Carefulness in Companionship
3. Tuesday: Purity in Sexuality
4. Wednesday: Diligence at Work
5. Thursday: Control of One's Speech
6. Friday: Simplicity of Lifestyle
7. Saturday: Love for the Less Fortunate

Sunday: Meditate on any of these verses from Proverbs on **humility**: 1:7; 3:34; 8:13; 9:10; 11:2; 14:12, 26, 27; 15:25, 33; 16:5, 6, 18, 19; 18:12; 19:23; 21:4, 24, 29; 22:4; 23:17; 28:14; 29:23.

Monday: Meditate on any of these verses from Proverbs on **right companionship**: 1:10-19; 11:14; 12:26; 14:7; 15:22; 16:19; 18:24; 20:18-19; 21:16; 22:5, 24; 23:20-21; 24:1, 2, 6, 21; 28:7; 29:3, 12, 24.

Tuesday: Meditate on any of these verses from Proverbs on **sexual purity**: 2:16-19; 5:1-23; 6:24-35; 7:1-27; 11:29; 13:22, 24; 23:27-28; 31:3, 30.

Wednesday: Meditate on any of these verses from Proverbs on **diligence at work**: 6:6-11; 10:5; 12:11, 14b, 24, 27; 13:4; 14:23; 18:9; 19:24; 20:4, 13; 24:27, 30-34; 27:18; 28:19.

Thursday: Meditate on any of these verses from Proverbs on **control of one's speech**: 10:18-21; 11:13; 12:16; 13:3; 14:29; 15:1-2, 4, 7, 18, 28; 16:13, 21, 24, 28, 32; 17:7, 9; 18:2, 4, 6-7, 13, 19, 20-21; 19:11; 20:15; 24:26; 28:23; 29:5, 8, 11, 20, 22; 30:10, 32, 33.

Friday: Meditate on any of these verses from Proverbs on **simplicity of lifestyle**: 3:9, 10; 11:4, 16, 28; 13:8, 11; 15:16-17, 27; 16:8; 17:1; 21:17; 22:1, 7b; 23:1-5, 20, 21; 28:6, 11, 20, 22, 25; 30:8-9.

Saturday: Meditate on any of theses verse from Proverbs on **helping the less fortunate**: 3:27-28; 11:16-17, 24-25, 30; 14:21, 31; 15:27; 17:5; 21:13; 22:9, 16, 22-23; 24:11; 28:8, 22, 27; 29:7, 14; 31:8, 9.

By studying and thinking about a particular pillar of wisdom on a given day of the week, you will more readily recall and retain the seven pillars of wisdom as a whole. Along with using a weekly schedule, the author recommends that you keep a wisdom journal in which you daily track your efforts at incorporating more wisdom into your life.

Lastly, daily prayer is crucial for developing greater wisdom in general and humility in particular. Through prayer, the individual learns to slow down and get in contact with the source of all life—God the Father. Prayer allows the individual to become less self-absorbed and more in tune with spiritual pursuits. Prayer is the ultimate spiritual exercise, bringing us back to the first pillar of wisdom, humility.

To pray is to humble yourself, genuinely seeking God with an open heart.

Appendix J:
A Memory System for Obtaining Greater Wisdom

Below is a memory strategy for the seven principles of wisdom. By associating each principle of wisdom with (1) a number, (2) a rhyming word, and (3) a sentence, you can more readily remember the seven pillars of wisdom. Use the following strategy to help stimulate daily awareness of the seven pillars of wisdom.

(Pillar 1: humility)
1. one/gun: With a <u>humble heart</u>, I gave the robber with the *gun* everything he wanted.

(Pillar 2: carefulness in companions)
2. two/shoe: I would rather walk with only one shoe in <u>the company of the wise</u> than with two *shoes* in the company of the foolish.

(Pillar 3: Sexual Purity)
3. three/tree: Like an immovable and fruitful *tree* is the <u>faithful and loyal spouse</u>.

(Pillar 4: Diligence)
4. four/door: <u>Hard work</u> is the *door* that opens into prosperity and personal satisfaction.

(Pillar 5: Carefulness in Speech)
5. five/hive: Like the bees of a *hive*, <u>communicate to others that which is constructive for the whole of the community</u>.

(Pillar 6: Simplicity of Life Style)
6. six/wick: A little candle with a <u>small, simple</u> *wick* that sheds light is better than a large lighthouse with a burned out bulb.

(Pillar 7: Compassion to Others)
7. seven/heaven: *Heaven* on earth is realized in a life of <u>service to others</u>.

You are encouraged to develop your own memory system to help you recall the seven pillars of wisdom. By developing your own system to remember and meditate on these essential principles of wisdom, you will increase the likelihood of using them.

Suggestion for the Youth Pastor

Have the youth in your group read one chapter each week. Questions for the chapter also should be answered. At your next meeting, discuss the particular pillar of wisdom that the youth group is studying for the week. Did anything in the chapter stand out to them? Next, discuss the questions, eliciting responses from the youth. Point out the practical benefits of a particular principle of wisdom being discussed. Be sure to add your own responses (self-disclosure) to help the youth group feel comfortable in sharing. Share with the group how a particular pillar of wisdom has been beneficial to you.

Selected Resources

The American Heritage Dictionary of the English Language. Boston, New York: Houghton Mifflin Company, 1982, 1985, and 1991.

The Holy Bible, New Century Version. Nashville: Thomas Nelson, Inc., 2005.

Fry, Ron. *How to Study.* 6th edition. Delmar Cengage Learning; 6th edition, 2004

Kaplan, Justin, ed.. *Bartlett's Familiar Quotations.* 17th edition. Boston, New York, and London: Little, Brown and Company, 2002.

The Oxford Dictionary of Quotations. 6th edition. New York: Oxford University Press, USA, 1966.

Pfeiffer, Charles F., Vos, Howard F and Rea, John, eds., *Wycliffe Bible Encyclopedia.* Chicago: Moody Press, 1975.

Thomas, Robert L., ed. *New American Standard Exhaustive Concordance of the Bible.* Nashville: Holman, 1981.

CPSIA information can be obtained at www.ICGtesting.com
Printed in the USA
LVOW13s2355310114

371887LV00001B/3/P